DECOUPAGE
A Limitless World in Decoration

For
Marilyn Hagen
who proved herself a
friend even tho'
a stranger —
with deepest appreciation,
and always my best wishes

Dorothy Hassower

July 10/59 —

Frontispiece "Niche and Corridor," fantasy in decoupage by Carl Federer

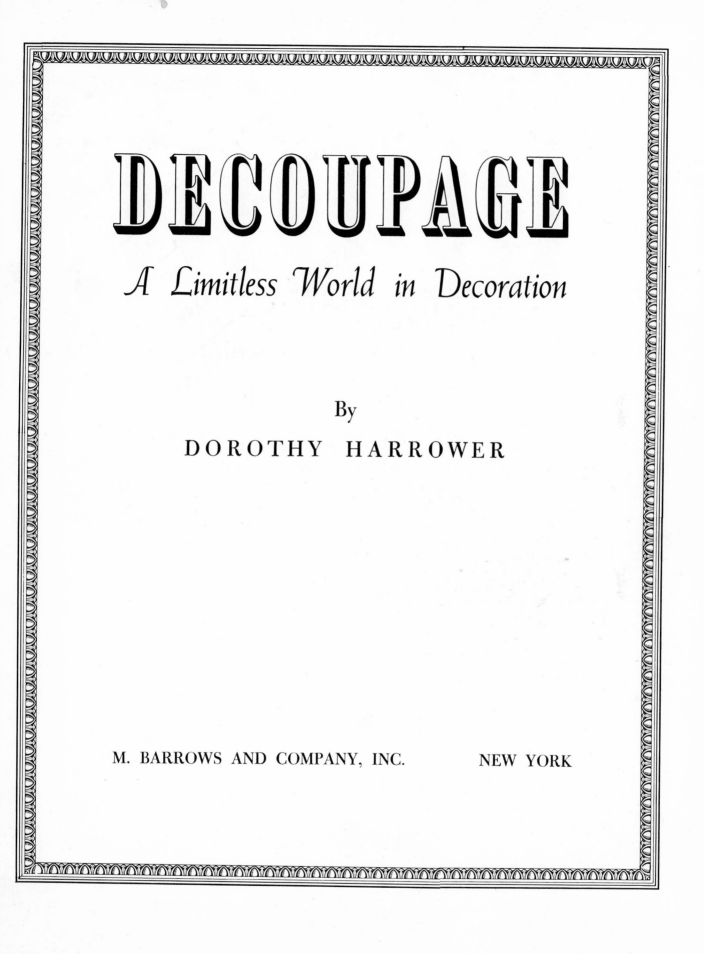

DECOUPAGE

A Limitless World in Decoration

By

DOROTHY HARROWER

M. BARROWS AND COMPANY, INC.   NEW YORK

Dedicated To

My Husband

PAT

His was the magic of believing in me.

Acknowledgments

A stage setting evokes little interest without talented persons to give meaning to the language and action necessary to make a play come alive. So when I started casting about for a quiet place to put my voluminous notes in shape, my good friend Jane Scriven turned over her New Hampshire house to me for the purpose. Later when I needed someone to edit the book Miss Scriven introduced me to Mary Lyon.

Years of searching could not have produced a person better qualified or more sympathetic to the subject. Mrs. Lyon's years as editor of one of the outstanding craft magazines in this country, *Craft Horizons,* gave her a special insight which the book required.

Her personal interest far exceeded her interest as an editor for she did much research on her own. To say that she enhanced the book is an understatement. She made it.

Cap Laroe and Albert Waks both contributed wonderful photography entirely on their own and spent precious hours to do so.

Calvin S. Hathaway, director of Cooper Union Museum for the Arts of Decoration, a friend of many years, has never failed to encourage me in my research and studies in the field. Members of the staff at Cooper Union Museum, Hedy Backlin, keeper of decorative arts, and Jean Mailey, formerly assistant curator in the Department of Textiles both gave me invaluable help, as did Dr. Richard Paul Wunder, keeper of the prints.

I am also indebted to Edward Croft-Murray, keeper of prints at the British Museum, as well as to A. Hyatt Mayor, curator of prints at the Metropolitan Museum of Art.

Mr. Mayor has happily provided a foreword, and in doing so has given the book the finishing touch which only he could give.

To each one of this talented company I give my most heartfelt thanks.

So now let us ring up the curtain.

DOROTHY HARROWER

Introduction

Decoupage—the art of cutting out and of pasting up cutouts for decoration—has, under one name or another, for centuries fascinated the artists, artisans and even peasants of many cultures. Yet little has been written about it. The purpose of this book is to reveal the world of decoupage to the uninitiated, to explain what it is and how it's done. From a wealth of experience, Dorothy Harrower here points the way to the pursuit of decoupage for fun or for profit and without undue stress or needless failures.

Because the subject is wide, the book has been divided into three parts, making it easy for the reader to turn to the particular aspect of decoupage that interests him. Part I includes, among other things, the definitions and antecedents of decoupage; in Part II Mrs. Harrower expertly analyzes a number of widely varied projects in decoupage; and in Part III she deals with methods, materials, tools and special techniques.

It should be clear to every reader of this unique book that there is no intention to set hard and fast rules for producing a work of art. Even the mechanics of making a good decoupage are entirely flexible — as they are relatively simple. Moreover, everyone who practices this craft devises his own pet methods and short cuts. The author is fully aware that each one will go his own way, making his own discoveries and also his own mistakes. This is part of the satisfaction of creating an original decoupage or any other work of art. One can go all out sentimental, abstract nonobjective, or stick to purest circus — just so the result is one's personal achievement.

The Publishers

9

Contents

PART III

The Craft of Decoupage — Materials and Methods

Foreword

One of my learned friends once told me that at a certain moment in the eighteenth century all of the seven electoral princes of Germany spent their spare time turning ivory goblets — and the world was at peace. If Mrs. Harrower's book can absorb enough influential people in the practice of cutwork, she will have given mankind a document more precious than the charter of the United Nations.

Cutwork is international and has a long history. Before the Egyptians had scissors they composed decorations of bright leathers; and paper has been intricately snipped as far away as Bali and China. In the sixteenth century the Turkish paper cutters were important enough to organize themselves into a guild. The far-flung story can be followed in various parts of the Metropolitan Museum, which has a treasure of eighteenth- and nineteenth-century cutwork and silhouettes from the bequests of two remarkable collectors, Mary Martin and Glenn Tilley Morse. While these collectors particularly pursued silhouettes, and got work by almost every important maker of them, they did not neglect the elegant and spidery art of cutwork.

Scissors in a modern hand can perform as wonderfully as the knife of the intarsia worker during the Renaissance. Even you and I with perseverance can sublimate scraps of paper into decorations that will astonish us ourselves. So sharpen your scissors! Your country expects you to attempt the impossible — or at least to achieve the unbelievable. But stay your hand at prints of value, and do not imitate that Victorian lady who destroyed a folio of Audubon birds by shellacking them to screens.

A. Hyatt Mayor

Part I
The Arts of Decoupage and Collage

1. *L'arte del povero* secretary, Venice, *c.* 1730

CHAPTER 1

Defining Decoupage and Collage

A DECOUPAGE means a cutout.

A collage means a paste-up.

Obviously, both terms include the twin process of cutting out and pasting up, and refer to pictures or decoration made by pasting up pieces of cutout paper or other material.

Decoupage is a decorative art or craft which may have originated in France in the late seventeenth century. It consisted of decorating a box, a chest, a screen with colorful pasted cutouts to simulate painted surfaces. In Italy, it was called *l'arte del uomo povero,* the poor man's art; those who couldn't afford to have an artist paint furniture for them could get the same sumptuous effect with decoupage (see Plates 1 and 19). Decoupage can also refer to shadow boxes or pictures, also made from cutouts. And here is where you may stub your toe later unless you are prepared to skip lightly over, for there are areas, inevitably, where decoupage and collage overlap, a sort of no man's land where one man's collage approximates another's decoupage.

Collage is new. It is explicitly of the twentieth century. A collage, in the world of fine art, refers specifically to the painter's statement, an easel "painting" not necessarily of oils or water colors, but of cutout papers or fragments of other material—or a painting which at least incorporates these (see Plate 2). Aesthetically and categorically, it has nothing to do with decoupage except its "eccentricity of technique," as one critic has put it. Collage embraces montage and photomontage also,

2. "Merz," 1925, collage
by Kurt Schwitters

both forms of the same curious and diverting medium. Montage means a "mounting." It's a collage of presumably identifiable subjects, set up in a pleasing or a startling composition. It may incorporate cutout elements or it may not. In common with other expressions of collage, it frequently includes three-dimensional objects, or things that "cast a shadow"—such things as buttons, keys, nails, and any number of other improbable and incongruous scraps that nevertheless combine to speak their piece. A photomontage is a collage of photographs, or a painting incorporating photographic material.

All the words designating cutouts and paste-ups are French words without English equivalents. And interestingly enough, few of these words are in the

3. *Découpure* in white on blue by Marie-Antoinette *c.* 1780

dictionaries, English or French, as identified with this art. Collage, for example, is defined in the French dictionary as the hanging of wallpaper. The English dictionary by-passes the word decoupage. There is one French word, however, which was used to describe cutouts for ornament in the eighteenth century: that word was *découpure*. It was used by Marie-Antoinette to describe the lacy, valentinelike memento she cut with her own hands (Plate 3). It occurs from time to time in the literature of the day. Literally translated it means "a thing cut out; cut paper work."

4. Silhouette of the Clinton family, New York, 1839, by Edouart, the French silhouettist

To be sure, *découper* means to cut out, but rather in the sense of "to carve as a fowl, or woodwork"; or it means a mechanical stamping out. *Découpage* and *découpure*, on the other hand, are both used to describe the indentation of the shores of island or seacoast. In eighteenth-century England, decoupage was called "japanning," with the emphasis on the application of the outer coats of varnish or lacquer.

Few art or craft forms have as many names to classify them, their various styles and techniques. Each name suggests its own particular genre and, in some cases, the period when it was popular.

A case in point is the silhouette, another sort of cutout, a shadow picture, the precursor of photography and therefore doomed to a short-lived vogue. Although some exquisite arrangements have been devised by silhouettists (see Plate 4) it doesn't qualify as true decoupage, since the image to be cut out, trapped mechanically by light, is complete in itself and does not require the redesigning essential in putting together a decoupage. Also it is essentially portraiture, not decoration. Silhouette took its name from Etienne de Silhouette, minister of finance in France in the eighteenth century. Because of his penurious policies toward the poor, his name went into the language—and into the dictionary—deridingly: *à la silhouette* meant getting a portrait the cheap way, without paying an artist to paint it.

5. *Trompe l'oeil* screen-mural by Rita Boley Bolaffio

6. Surrealist arrangement of sand and shells by William Harris

A better example, possibly, of a specialized—and dated—form of decoupage is potichomania: an eighteenth- to nineteenth-century craze in France and England for pasting color cutouts on the inside of glass vessels to imitate Oriental vases, Sèvres, and other porcelains too costly for the average genteel lady's pocketbook.

HOW TO TELL THE DIFFERENCE

It takes a certain mental agility to tell a collage from a decoupage in those areas where they inevitably overlap, as in pictures to hang on the wall. There is no difficulty in recognizing one of Schwitters' "Merz" as a collage (Plate 2), nor in spotting a Bolaffio mural (Plate 5), as decoupage. It's the borderline cases that have you guessing. The puzzle presents itself when William Harris chooses to make a collage depicting a surrealist arrangement of cutout shells on a desert floor (Plate 6); and

7. "Confederate Money," collage-montage by Carl Federer

DECOUPAGE

Carl Federer composes a fantasy called "Niche and Corridor" (see frontispiece) and declares unequivocally that it's decoupage. "Confederate Money," he says with equal forthrightness, is a collage-montage (Plate 7).

YOU NAME IT

It becomes immediately apparent that the widest latitude is permissible in defining cutouts and paste-ups. Possibly the artist who knows the exact intent of his composition is best qualified to classify it. At an exhibition of twentieth-century German paintings in the autumn of 1957 at the Museum of Modern Art in New York, one small room was given to collages. In describing Max Ernst's collages, Werner Haftman says: "In these *montages* one basic aim of veristic Surrealism was already achieved." (Italics are ours.) Here a critic instinctively used the word "montage" because to him these looked like montages.

There is no occasion here for a battle of semantics. Since the lexicographers have virtually ignored this phase of art and decoration, the field is wide open for you to make your own distinctions and attach your own meanings. And you may be as precise about it or as free as you choose. When the dictionaries get around to it, it is you who will have done the groundwork for them in evolving their definitions.

Broadly speaking, a collage is a painter's original concept composed of paint, papers and other materials to make an effect, evoke a mood; it is often abstract or nonobjective. A decoupage is representative, embodying cutouts that are redesigned to depict a scene, to re-create a period, to tell a story or to decorate a plain surface.

TRY THIS EXERCISE

Suppose you find yourself strolling through a gallery of collages—at least on the catalogue it says "Exhibition of Collages." One of them, made of wooden blocks, newspaper cutouts and wire, stands out as tortured and contrived. You can't say just why, but it's fairly repellent to you. Another is pleasing, even exciting, a challenge in counterpoise of shapes and colors. None is altogether meaningless. Suddenly you find yourself confronted by a montage: it's dramatic, a medley of bright colors. Now, why did you call it a montage?

"Well," you say to yourself, "it looks like a montage. 'Montage' means a 'mounting,' doesn't it? What's it supposed to be? Why it's book jackets!" you perceive, peering closer. "How clever," you say to yourself, "I like that."

Presently you are arrested by a small picture that seems fairly to leap from its frame—cutout shapes like twisted treetops in a storm, glaring white spaces, a sky split by zigzag lightning, brilliant and artificial.

"It looks as though they'd used Lurex," you find, with your nose practically in it. "And pieces of tin, cut jagged with scissors . . . and something that looks like ground glass. I couldn't have believed that one small decoupage could explode in my face like that. . . . It has the kick of an El Greco . . . in miniature."

Well, you named it. You called it a decoupage, and so it was one as far as you're concerned. Chances are the artist who composed it also called it a decoupage.

It is possible that the difference between these pictures, a collage, a montage and a decoupage, lies in your perception of it. And is it, anyhow, a matter of such colossal importance? A rose by any other name is a rose is a rose is a rose.

CHAPTER 2

The Fine Art of Collage

THE WORD COLLAGE, then connotes the world of fine arts, the painter's world. It describes or classifies pictures into which pieces of foreign, often incongruous, material have been incorporated, such as textured fabric, paper of all kinds, lace, straw, and bits of old broken wood. The list of substances is endless, the results provocative.

It all started as a revolt. Certain painters took up collage to underline their break with the conventional strictures imposed by what seemed to them to be outworn art forms. They felt that something new could be said by a picture, and that substances other than oils or water colors could say it.

Collage dates from around 1912. It crept into the revolution in painting and sculpture on the heels of cubism at the end of the first decade of this century. Pablo Picasso (see plate 8) and Georges Braque were probably responsible for it; who was first is not certain. It may have been Picasso with his "Still Life with Chair Caning," which was a painting in oil on canvas, with pasted linoleum simulating chair caning.

Braque and Picasso combined oil or gouache on canvas or on wood, charcoal or pencil drawings, with bits of paper, torn newspaper, string, plaster, sand and other things. Picasso called his *papiers collés* (pasted papers), in order to differentiate them from the collages of the Dadaists, a group of rebels who emerged during World War I and with whom he had little sympathy, although he had tremendous influence on their work. Juan Gris was another painter who made early experiments with collage.

8. "Pipe, Glass, Bottle of Rum," Paris, 1914. Collage by Pablo Picasso.

Dada was an international eruption which seems to have started in New York and in Zurich, Switzerland, around 1916. The Dadaists embraced collage with frenzy. With it and their antirational paintings they mocked the "shams" of earlier European culture, sometimes with bitter iconoclasm, sometimes with sly humor, tongue in cheek. The movement spread rapidly in Europe after the war.

Jean Arp, the painter, helped found Dadaism in Zurich in 1916. His collages were characteristically made with bits of paper in geometric arrangements, sometimes torn instead of cut. Arp went along with the Dadaists in Cologne of whom Max Ernst was a founder. Ernst, a virtuoso in many methods, later was called the foremost master of surrealist collage (see plate 9). From Cologne Dada moved on to Hanover, Berlin and Paris where eventually it died in the 1920's.

From the ashes of Dada sprang surrealism, an art movement of deep

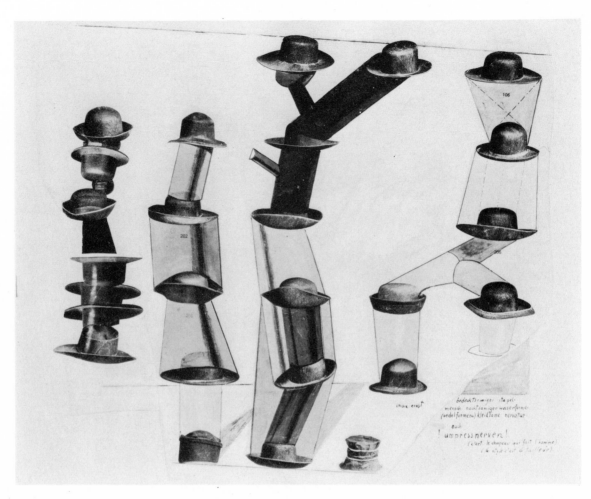

9. "The Hat Makes the Man,"
   collage by Max Ernst, 1920

consequence. Many of the early surrealists were ex-Dadaists—Arp, Man Ray, Ernst—who continued to make collages, but only as a digression from their more serious paintings of the fantasy world, man's unconscious mind which, they held, was the essential source of art. They breathed life and meaning into their paper cutouts. Through symbolism they revealed the stuff of man's subconscious—his pleasures, his conflicts, and all the many hidden workings of his inmost being.

Juan Miró early became identified with the surrealists; shortly after, Tanguy, Magritte and others followed and, about 1929, Salvador Dali. The surrealists claimed such artists as di Chirico, Klee, Duchamp, Picasso, who in reality were independents. Picasso's interest in his *papiers collés* had become intermittent after the war but revived in 1924, and toward 1936 he had grown more and more involved with the surrealist painters greatly influencing Miró and Dali.

The surrealists assembled various materials, related or incongruous, and composed abstractions that developed an idea, suggested a mood, or captured a moment in memory. None of their work was factual in that one could glance at it quickly and catch the familiar. These pictures had to be examined carefully—and then weren't always soul-shattering. But they very often left the beholder with a sense of the wonder of simple things, an appreciation of the form the artist had given them, and the rather arresting realization that things small as these still had the power to make a final statement.

It is interesting to note that the placement and composition of these fragments of daily living embody the principle of all good art: law and order. Each torn piece is torn that way with a purpose, for each piece must conform to the space it occupies and in so doing support the materials that surround it. Its shape must be pleasing to the eye and supplement its relation to the whole. In short, the creator of a collage is using succinct symbols to capture a reality without presenting the thing itself. Looking at a good collage is like interpreting poetry—one reads between the lines. In more comprehensive terms collage can be explained this way:

"Collage cannot be defined adequately as merely a technique of cutting and pasting, for its significance lies not in its technical eccentricity but its relevance to two basic questions which have been raised by twentieth century art: the nature of reality and the nature of painting itself. Collage has been the means through which the artist incorporates reality in the picture without imitating it."*

CONTEMPORARY COLLAGE

In the last decade interest in collage has increased notably among artists both in the United States and abroad. During World War II several young Americans painting in abstract style began to use collage as a medium; to those who have grown up in the traditions of abstract and nonobjective painting it has proved an obvious and diverting mode of expression. In France Henri Matisse began experimenting with his *papiers découpés* (paper cutouts) in 1946. Many of the major compositions of his last years were in paper rather than in oil. He brought enormous

---

* Excerpt from a publication issued by the Museum of Modern Art in New York, 1948, on the occasion of its first comprehensive exhibition of collage.

29

prestige to the field. At the exhibition in the Museum of Modern Art in 1948 virtually all of the great in collage were represented, except Matisse, whose experiments were not available at that time.

In February, 1956, the Rose Feld Gallery in New York presented the International Collage Exhibition, showing twenty-six "early modern masters" from Europe, beginning with Arp. Twenty-eight young Americans were included, and others from France, Germany, Belgium, Italy, Switzerland and England totaled some eighty entrants.

A baker's dozen of Picasso's *papiers collés,* from 1911 to 1926, were hung at the Picasso 75th Anniversary Exhibition at the Museum of Modern Art during the summer of 1957. And in the autumn, at the exhibition of twentieth-century German painters, collages by Max Ernst, Arp and Schwitters drew special attention.

From mid-December into January, 1958, the Zabriskie Gallery in New York presented an important anthology of American collage. Of the sixty or more painters showing, a number have achieved authentic expression in collage as a medium. Among these were Esteben Vicente, Hans Moller, Robert Motherwell, Franz Kline, Sue Fuller, Ilse Getz, Jean Xceron, Arthur B. Dove, Corrado Marca-Relli and others. The exhibition bears out a current trend, in collage of the abstract and non-objective schools, to simulate painting.

This same drift was evident in the one-man show of collages by Charles Sorel at the Sagittarius Gallery, New York, during January, 1958. Using torn papers of every kind and color, Mr. Sorel with infinite patience and skill builds up vivid pictures, impressionistic but frankly representational: still lifes and street scenes (see Plate 10).

A MASTER OF COLLAGE

Kurt Schwitters, one of the artists to take up collage early, stands out as one of the great. From Hanover, Schwitters made his first collages at the end of World War I. He was sympathetic with the Dadaists at Zurich, particularly Arp, but found himself sharply at odds with Dadaism in Germany, aesthetically and politically. Like Picasso, he gave his collages a special name in order to dissociate his work from Dada. Schwitters made up the word "Merz"—meaning "life's little nothings," perhaps?

10. "Street Scene in Venice," collage by Charles Sorel

—and for a time published an art magazine under that title. "Merz" was the second syllable of what was possibly his first collage, "Commerz" ("Commerce"), pasted in 1918, and incorporating paper, wood, cardboard, corrugated paper and cloth.

As a young man, Schwitters chose to quit his native Germany for England. For years he muddled along, writing nonsense tales for the Hanover daily newspaper under such titles as "The Private Life of a Street Car" and "The Public Auction Sale of a Menagerie"—delightful fantasies that paid the rent. Slowly, out of his toil, came recognition. It burst fully upon him just before he died in 1948.

A first look at Schwitters' collages may leave one unmoved. Only after thoughtful scrutiny does their impact come through. His was the work of the true artist, his the mind that collects the commonplace and makes of it a provocative, personal statement. Old theater tickets, scraps of colored paper, perhaps torn from a program, and other bits of the discarded take on a touching charm and set a mood that cannot lightly be dismissed. Further study of the materials he used, how he used them, will do much to open the mind and create an appreciation of the wonder of the simple things that lie at hand.

Form was of paramount importance to Schwitters: first, the outside form to be filled, and then the form of things arranged within it. He composed and built up with line, color, shape and texture, all laid one against another. He believed that freedom was achieved through discipline, as is true of every form of art. Schwitters had the integrity, staying power and belief in himself that the discipline of drudgery and hard work gave him. He expressed it through his deep respect for the fragments of life which he used for his compositions. The humbler they were, the more importance he gave them in the scheme of things. He created a respect for the castoff and the discarded, not for themselves so much as for what they once had been. His were not the gleanings of a magpie mind, but the ordered and telling placement of interesting, once useful things that made his art in collage most arresting.

The two examples of Schwitters' work chosen are widely different, yet in their essence they uphold his regard for the small, the fragile and the commonplace.

"Merz 22," 1920 (Plate 11), is a record of his daily living while still in Europe. It is composed of railroad and bus tickets, wallpaper and ration stamps—an eloquent statement of life in Germany during World War I. The queuing up for food

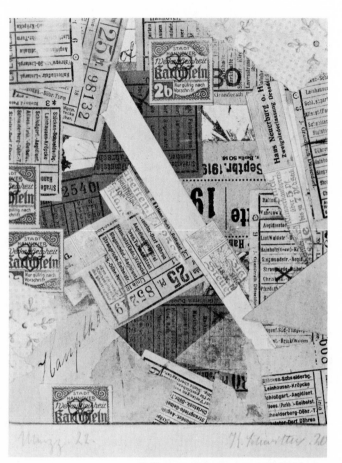

11. "Merz. 22," collage
by Kurt Schwitters, 1920

doled out through ration stamps is something not easily dismissed from human experience. Nor were the crowded trains and the jammed buses of that time. Wallpaper symbolized a place of retreat where one could rest and gather strength for the next grinding day of toil. The demanding straight and narrow path dominates the composition, as indeed it did that existence. Thin pieces of carefully cut tissue paper veil an area here and there; and watermarks, gentle reminders of the rain in which one stood waiting, eternally waiting, remain.

"Merz" (with lace paper), 1925, is a recording of gayer things and happier times (Plate 2). It is composed of colored paper, lace paper and the paper top of a cigarette box. It exhales gaiety, lightheartedness, warmth of color and the fun and femininity of lace. The cigarettes are sociable. This delightful collage tells of a pleasant moment, relaxed and free from the pressures of life. Simply and skillfully, Schwitters has captured it.

12. Italian monastery, collage by William Harris

EXAMPLES OF AMERICAN COLLAGE

The work of artists in this field, Americans of widely diverse talent, illustrates the depth and scope for individual expression inherent in the medium of collage. This is in no sense a comprehensive review of collage in America. These few have been chosen, rather, for variety of idiom and method.

William Harris is a master of different forms. A New Yorker active in the field of design, Mr. Harris likes to create his own textured papers, an example of which is shown (Plate 12). This is a simple process, technically known as "working wet." For the mottled effect a thin, cheap quality of paper is best. It is thoroughly wet first, then crumpled. Next it is spread out on a glass surface and the back painted with Higgins' ink, full tone. The color seeps through the creases and gives the appearance of ancient fresco. Finally, the paper is flattened out on a dry glass surface and allowed to dry out completely.

Using this textured paper, Mr. Harris built his picture of what looks like an old fort or an Italian hill town or monastery. The entire picture was carried out in shades of beige. He placed cutouts for roofs, doors, windows and shadows, with color accent indicating people in the foreground. The outline of the roofs, towers, outside walls and the building seen in the distance were all separate cutouts. The result is a restful architectural compilation. One feels that one could go, along with the monks, through the great gates on the right hand and lose oneself in a contemplative garden.

Clever arrangement and use of textured fabrics distinguish the collages in Plates 13 and 14. One need not see the shore upon which the small sandpipers are busily searching for food (Plate 13); it is all quite explicit. The arrangement, the placement of each bird, gives a sense of direction and action. It is amusing to know that they were made out of scraps of material, with toothpicks for feet and bills and mounted on a piece of woven fabric.

The picture in Plate 14 is put together with a piece of woven matting for the sombrero, lace for its band and a striped woven fabric for the serape. Brilliant red, black and gray are the decorative accents. The fun and story in this single figure is that by itself it suggests a group of men enjoying a pleasant game of cards in a simple taberna somewhere in South America.

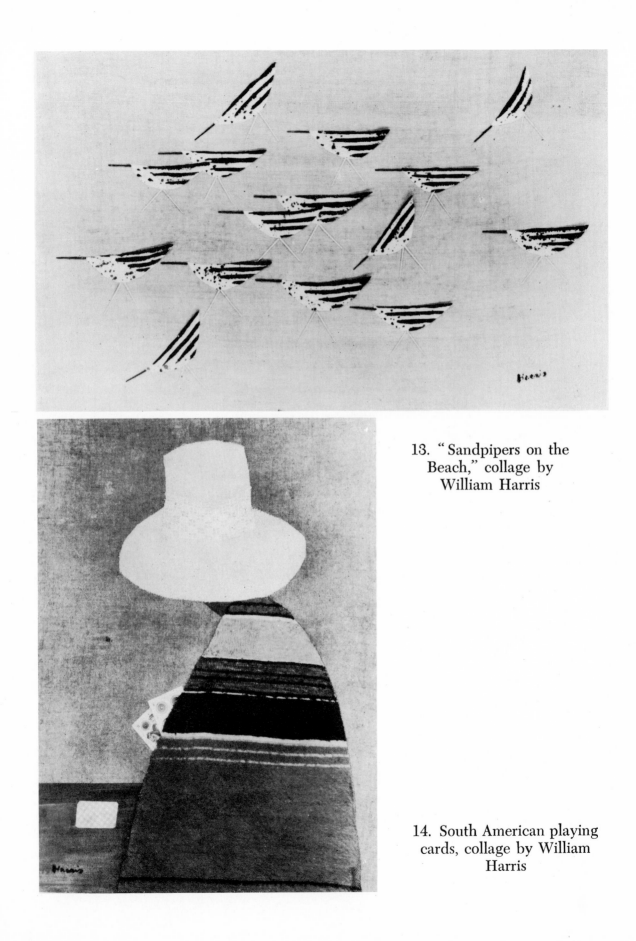

13. "Sandpipers on the
Beach," collage by
William Harris

14. South American playing
cards, collage by William
Harris

Both of these were composed of negligible bits of this and that—castoffs from the old rag bag, little nothings that became big somethings.

From the world of fantasy is the collage in Plate 6; the enlarged color-print shells rest upon an ocean floor from which springs a razor-sharp mountain. All is enchantment, all a bit unreal.

Robert Courtright, who grew up in the South and came to New York to study, lives now in the south of France, where he works and prepares for showing in various exhibitions of paintings. His work attests his enjoyment of the architectural; in Europe he has found it an inspiration and a never-ending stimulus. Plates 15 and 16 illustrate this, for each one is different from the other in concept and execution.

Working with paper, he gets his textural contrast by painting his surfaces, then cutting them out and mounting them. "Iglesia" (Castile)—Plate 15—is a carefully drawn plan upon which levels of light and shade have been imposed by means of the paper cutout. The decorative façade suggests the grandeur of a Spanish cathedral, and the blocked-in areas in the foreground the plaza that surrounds it. The door itself is a cutout placed behind the pillars. Mr. Courtright's excellent distribution of intense black is noteworthy. He takes one right into the cathedral, for as one looks at it, the door almost opens and one finds oneself immersed in the mystery of the fabulous interior.

"Tower, Badia a Settimo" (Tuscany)—Plate 16—is another example of Courtright's skill with paper and painted texture. The arched windows of the tower are all cut out and pasted on a plain piece of paper; true, also, of the altarpiece resting over the door. Again his distribution of darks is masterly; none detracts from the altarpiece. The altarpiece is the tower of strength in the picture, the focal point for the soul. One can kneel without entering.

Mr. Courtright's pieces are all executed in subtle colors. They do not jar one, for they have a gentle quality. An appreciation of his fine, thoughtful craftsmanship, of well-integrated values, grows on the viewer. And if one has seen the places he pictures, his works evoke enchanted memories.

A new collage by Sue Fuller, known for her abstract string composi-

15. "Iglesia," Castile. Collage by Robert Courtright.

16. "Tower, Badia a Settimo," Tuscany. Collage by Robert Courtright.

17. "Waraku Odori," folk festival in Japan. Collage by Sue Fuller.

tions, evidences a sensitive and vigorous use of the medium. "Waraku Odori" (Plate 17), celebrating an autumn folk festival in Japan, is built up of the festival's program, a *kabuki* or theater ticket, gay matchbox covers, fibrous and patterned papers and the skeletonized leaves which the Japanese dye and use for bookmarkers. She has invested it with delicate harmonies of green, lavender and white.

Two artists in decoupage have almost simultaneously put together collage-montages which by some odd coincidence have great similarity of subject, and both sing a song of sixpence.

"Confederate Money" is the name of the collage by Carl Federer (Plate 7). It was a commission for a collage picture to be hung in a man's library. It was to

18. "Money," collage-montage by Rita Boley Bolaffio

re-create in spirit and manner a painting by William Harnett, nineteenth-century American still-life painter. Harnett specialized in Confederate money and related subjects, adding such *trompe l'oeil* (fool the eye) effects as a pipe going out, emitting dying wisps of smoke. The bonds in "Confederate Money" are real, also the keys and the cards. All else is faked with paper cutouts including the watch and chain.

Rita Bolaffio has called her composition "Money" (Plate 18). It is an ingenious combination of real objects, cutouts from old prints and sheer illusion in paper. It has a highly colored background in rusty textured papers, scraps of gold and colored tinsel. The dollar signs are made of gold paper pasted over cardboard, the Stock Exchange report is cut from the newspaper. The key, the wallet, the bills and coins are real. An amusing device is the machine, cut from an old print, with a bar of silver being fed into it and minted coins falling out below. The stamping machine and the pistol also are cut from prints. It is interesting that Mrs. Bolaffio, with a flair for brilliant, realistic display and *trompe l'oeil* magic, should find it fun to contrive a painter's witty abstract statement.

"Street Scene in Venice" (Plate 10), a collage by Charles Sorel, captures the effect of an impressionistic oil painting through the clever application of an infinite number of torn scraps of paper of many kinds: tissue paper, writing paper in various weights, wrapping paper, tracing paper—anything that suits Mr. Sorel's purpose for building an effect of shading, texture, transparency or opacity. Occasionally he dyes or colors a bit for special accent. The walls of the houses in this scene are made from many-patterned, veined and marbled papers in shades of apricot fading into the grays, and the darker stretches of roughly paved street. The wash dancing in the breeze is mostly of different-textured writing papers, with some reds and pinks and a few darks. The coster in dark brown pants is pushing a cart of crimson flowers toward the deep blue Adriatic beneath a pale sky more green than blue. Balcony floors are made from many layers of black tissue paper, edged with single strips of white tissue to give them solidity and dimension. The varnish Mr. Sorel uses to protect his collages gives them a glowing, enamel-like, precise finish very pleasing to the eye. This will tone down with time, however, he says to contribute a rich, mellowing effect.

CHAPTER 3

The History and Antecedents of Decoupage

T<small>HE STORY</small> of decoupage has never been told. It is doubtful if ever it will be in its entirety. A reconstruction from seventeenth- and eighteenth-century pieces which have survived the vicissitudes of fire and flood and the depradations of time yields, at best, only fragmentary documentation.

It is probable that much that remains of decoupage from the seventeenth and through the nineteenth centuries is privately owned. Certainly it is rare in the museums of this country. There is still, however, a significant residue to be observed here: furniture from France and Italy; shadow boxes and pinprick pictures from all over the Continent; toy theaters from every country in Europe; the peep shows from England and the *vues d'optiques* from France; as well as countless decorated boxes, fans, screens and other small articles to be found in the antique shops and flea markets here and abroad.

A provocative clue to the early development of decoupage in Europe is provided by study of the spread of printing and prints after Gutenberg (*c.* 1450). For obviously, nobody thought of decorating surfaces with cutout pictures until suitable ones appeared; painting and various kinds of inlay had always served such purposes. True, there were color prints in Europe from the sixteenth century on, made from wood blocks. But these were chiefly of a religious character, like the early German image prints. Or they were such items as the first playing cards to be printed in Europe and the thirteenth-century printed textiles of Italy—hardly subject matter to spur the invention of a somewhat frivolous, if graceful, decorative art.

42

19. *L'arte del povero* Venetian secretary, *c.* 1700.
Turquoise, browns, reds.

A review of the progress of printing reveals, among other things, that Venice by the year 1500 led all European cities in printing. Before that date there had been 201 master printers in business there and an output of several million books. Illustrations in black, red and yellow appeared. It was an era of glory in Venice, with the spread of commerce across the world, the gold and treasures of the Orient pouring in, along with heavy shipments of paper by sea. It is thought that Venice during the sixteenth century may have become a major source of prints; so it is not surprising that decoupage, or *l'arte del uomo povero*, flourished there from the middle of the seventeenth century (see Plates 1 and 19), and possibly earlier.

A volume entitled *Mobili Veneziani Lacatti* (Venetian Lacquered Furniture), a recent reprint, published by Luigi Alfieri in Milan, illustrates the magnificent furniture of the period—cabinets, secretaries, commodes, chairs—decorated with cutout prints, lacquered and gilded, in a more lavish and rococo style than the French furniture which it possibly preceded. These specimens are now in the museums of Rome, Florence, Milan, Turin and Genoa. It seems probable that *l'arte del povero* was cradled in Venice, the work of artisans, and not improbable that it was on occasion palmed off as painted furniture—as is also quite possible of the furniture of later date in France and England. Although little remains—or is known—of popular, single-sheet prints from Venice, is it an implausible assumption that Venetian printers perceived a profitable advantage in supplying prints suitable for the practice of *l'arte del povero*?

For decoupage was more than a pastime at the French court, and a fashionable hobby in England during the eighteenth and nineteenth centuries. It was also a business, an adjunct of printing. It is not difficult to picture various printers in France, England and Germany poring over plates and presses, turning out prints for cutouts, for toy theaters and peep shows designed specially to bring out perspective. In Germany Martin Englebrecht (1684-1756) produced and had published many prints from copper plates for peep shows and for a great variety of decorative motifs. There are still to be found, at dealers in rare books, albums of Englebrecht's handiwork —birds, butterflies, animals, acrobats and many other figures. Not only were these beautifully hand-colored for the purpose, but in some instances were already cut out for the convenience of the paster, just as in the case of the English tinsel pictures (see Plate 20).

WEST'S, Theatrical Portraits.
No. 55.

Mr. C. KEMBLE, as PRINCE of WALES
In the Coronation, as performed
at the Theatre Royal Covent Garden.

Courtesy of The Cooper Union Museum

20. Tinsel picture of Mr. C. Kemble as Prince of Wales

In France, too, the flowering of decoupage was inevitably linked with prints and the artists of the period who designed with utmost taste in the spirit of the new décor. Among the favorites were Boucher, Redouté and Pillement. Jean Pillement, in particular, was prolific with his inventions. His chinoiseries are famous, as are his designs for *toiles* and for the silk looms of Lyon; his birds, flowers, foliage, arabesques and borders; the small vignettes of chateau and farmstead.

Decoupage, which remained popular in France into the nineteenth century, was not called decoupage (see Chapter 1) but *découpure.* (See cutout by Marie-Antoinette, Plate 3.) Jean François Marmontel, an essayist of that day, wrote: "He showed me scenery, in *découpure,* on sheets of white paper, in which perspective was observed with amazing skill."*

Yet decoupage, perhaps partly because of its French name, is supposed to have originated in France, despite the fact that the French did not use the term. However that may be, it there acquired a character which is quintessentially French— graceful, gay, charming in color, design and application. It influenced the style of de- coupage of the time in other countries as it continues to impress itself today.

Among the treasured relics from the courts of Louis XV and Louis XVI, and later of Louis Philippe, are screens, boxes, window shades, the backs of hair- brushes. Fans were favorites for decoupage with the ladies of the court who often pre- ferred silk and brocade cutouts to paper. At about this time fans in decoupage were brought from China, made, no doubt, for the French and British trade. These depicted delicate, colorful figures pasted on in outline in the rich brocades and textured silks of Chinese costumes. The faces also were pasted on, cutouts of ivory shaved to a thickness of about 1/64th of an inch. In a good state of preservation are French shadow boxes encasing memorial tributes—floral arrangements of paper flowers hand-colored and gold-embossed, against backgrounds appropriately painted in purple or mauve. They celebrated weddings in the same way, using white paper cutouts with gold.

"LADIES' AMUSEMENT"

In 1760, a large book called *Ladies' Amusement, or The Whole Art of Japanning Made Easy* appeared in London, printed for Robert Sayer, at the Golden

* *J'ai vu de lui des paysages en découpure sur des feuilles de papier blanc où la per- spective était observée avec un art prodi- gieux."*

Buck, opposite Fetter Lane in Fleet Street. This enterprising printer had got together fifteen hundred hand-colored designs etched on two hundred copper plates, all taken from various artists such as Pillement, Fenn, Hemerich, Hancock, June and others, with assortments of flowers, shells, insects, foliage, landscapes, boats, beasts, vases, borders, "for joining in groups or to be placed singly." All of this was expressly for cutting out and pasting, for decorating anything from "a superb cabinet to the smallest toilet article."

Mr. Sayer does not feel constrained to offer an apology for publishing this work, since it will "enable anybody though unacquainted with design to embellish a plain surface with ornament superior to those we purchase at so great expense from Indra and elsewhere." Furthermore, in addition to amusing the ladies, it will be greatly in aid of "porcelaine manufacturers and others depending upon design" for their wares.

There follow five pages of instruction for japanning, preceded by "directions for composition" in which the reader is very commendably enjoined to observe propriety in the combination of subjects: "If the scene be European, in the body of your design" put in "no exotic or preposterous object. . . . We have seen a butterfly supporting an elephant and things equally absurd." On the other hand, he concedes that a taste "for the grotesque prevails; wild connections between beasts with flowers, shells with birds" may be allowed. Next, a short homily on perspective — "at far edges put the smallest trees."

Instructions are divided in three parts. First, the background: the sizing of the wood, the selection of paint colors—ivory black is recommended most highly. Second, "the several objects you intend to use must be neatly cut round with sicsars or the sharp point of a knife," then turned over and "brushed on the back with strong gum water or thin paste." You are warned not to set cutouts on as though they were "tumbling"; for sure alignment you may draw on the background vertical lines, with pencil, to be removed later with a piece of "clean bread." And last comes the varnishing or japanning. Seven coats of varnish or "seedlac" are recommended, "12 are better still." And for a final polish, bright and lasting, a rubdown with rottenstone. At the very end are lists of formulas for making gums, glues, pastes, lacquers and all such items when not procurable at the shops.

21. Horse chestnut
from Mrs. Delany's Flora

22. Wood vetch

from Mrs. Delany's Flora

THE REMARKABLE MRS. DELANY

Mrs. Delany, *née* Mary Granville in England, 1700, was a serious artist and a great lady who moved with the very flower of fashion in the glittering round of aristocratic eighteenth-century London.* Witty herself, she was surrounded by the wits of Mayfair, a darling in court circles. Widowed when she was twenty-three, at the death of her first husband, the elderly Mr. Pendarves, she was pursued by a host of suitors, among them Dean Swift and Lord Baltimore.

Throughout this gay and romantic period she remained devoted to her painting and drawing and received no small acclaim. It is said she had instruction in drawing, at his own instance, from William Hogarth. When eventually she was married again, to Dean Delany, and moved to Delville, the Delany house at Dublin, she continued her work in oils, crayon, pastels and pen and ink. At Delville she began making shell collages, or "mosaics." Among her projects, she did a cornice for the ceiling of the dining room, formerly the chapel, using "real shells in the manner of modelled stucco" worked into garlands of flowers. Her shell mosaics resembled fine carvings.

Years later, again a widow and back in London, Mrs. Delany continued to paint and draw with aplomb, never so happy as at work. But it was not until the age of seventy-four that this astonishing woman discovered or invented, rather, her own form of decoupage which she called "paper mosaics." The word "decoupage" was not in English usage then; at that time it was called "japanning." In any case, this original device of Mrs. Delany's was unrelated to that. And it came about quite by accident, possibly because she always had had a passion for flowers and had made a study of botany (see Plate 21).

Here's the story, taken from the "Introductory" of *Mrs. Delany* by R. Brimley Johnson:

> Having a piece of Chinese paper on the table of bright scarlet, a geranium caught her eye of a similar colour, and taking her scissors she amused herself with cutting out each flower, by her eye, in the paper which resembled its hue; she laid the paper petals on a black ground, and was so pleased with the effect that she proceeded to cut out the calyx, stalks and leaves in shades of green, and pasted them down, and after she had completed a sprig of geranium in this way, the Duchess of Portland came in and

* *Mrs. Delany*, with an Introductory by R. Brimley Johnson. Published by Stanley Paul & Company, London, 1925: Mrs. Delany at Court & among the Wits, being the record of a great lady of genius in the art of living. "I have heard Burke say that Mrs. Delany was the highest bred woman in the world, and the woman of fashion of all ages."—Dr. Johnson.

exclaimed, "What are you doing with the geranium?" having taken the paper imitation for the real flower. Mrs. Delany answered her that "if the Duchess really thought it so like the original, a new work was begun from that moment."

From that day until her eighty-fifth birthday in 1785, when her "eyes were no longer able to direct her scissors," she completed a thousand of her paper mosaic Flora, of which Sir Joseph Banks, the great naturalist, said that he would venture to describe botanically any plant from Mrs. Delany's imitations without the least fear of committing an error. Horace Walpole in his *Anecdotes of Painting* praised her "new branch" of art for its precision and unparalleled truth; Sir Joshua Reynolds admired its harmony and brilliance.

Thus the Flora, perhaps Mrs. Delany's magnum opus, were completed. The flower pictures or paper mosaics (Plate 22), were mounted on Chinese paper, washed black, and slipped into ten calfbound ledger volumes. These have been in the possession of the British Museum since 1897. In her will, Mrs. Delany requested that twenty of the flowers in paper mosaic be presented to Queen Charlotte. These now are in the library of Windsor Castle.

For the Flora, Mrs. Delany used to "procure various coloured papers from Captains of vessels coming from China; and bought up odd pieces from the paper stainers in which the colours had run so as to secure extraordinary and unusual tints. . . . The [living] plants themselves were set up against a background of black paper, doubled in the form of a folding screen, to throw up the outlines, shadows and lights. Every detail was cut out separately, by eye, straight from the plant itself. The delicacy of the craftsmanship is incredible; with its clear and unhesitating outline, bold curves, the minutest variation in tint, the exact character of surface . . . the miraculous realism of the Flora is but one aspect of their Art. To turn over these thousand brilliant flower pictures is to gaze spellbound upon bold splashes of vivid colour, gossamer delicacy in vignette, strange line-harmonies we had supposed Japanese. The design of each is a triumph of artistic convention; the composition positively startles one by its daring anticipation of the most modern examples of decorative applied art—and every subtlety of an unerring instinct for perfect grouping and composition: everywhere life, truth and art. Since the petals, stamina, style and leaves, the lights, shades and tints were all

50

23. Unassembled parts of peep show: proscenium upper left, backdrop lower right. By Martin Englebrecht.

cut out and laid on in place; since the veinings of leaves and the ridges of stalks are super-imposed; they have a solidity or rotund depth which gives them a radiant vitality."* Mrs. Delany's technique, totally original with her, foreshadowed the methods of modern artists in decoupage. Cutting out basic forms from colored papers, rather than cutting out from prints, as was customary in her day, is precisely the device most frequently used today by skilled professionals such as Rita Bolaffio and Helen Watkins. The book *Ladies' Amusement*, with its fabulous collection of prints for cutting out, appeared in London in 1760, almost fifteen years before Mrs. Delany began,

* From the "Introductory" of *Mrs. Delany.*

24. Contraptions for *vues d'optiques* and peep shows—note one at lower right

abstractedly it would seem, to play with scissors and paper. But hers emerged as a very different technique from that of her period, and was an essentially modern one.

PEEP SHOWS

Peep shows, popular as toys in Europe in the nineteenth century, along with the miniature theaters and the French *vues d'optiques*, provide an interesting sidelight on the progress of decoupage. While all of these were not necessarily cutouts, some of them were. And all were specially printed for their several purposes. They offer today a rich source of material for decoupage in the traditional manner.

Peep shows were made in several countries and in a variety of subjects, dramatic or spectacular. In Germany, in the eighteenth century, Martin Englebrecht designed and published his share of these, as noted above, among them "The Flood" (Noah's), now at the Cooper Union Museum. The prints for these were made in sets (see Plate 23), cut out and arranged in a series, in a box somewhat like an elongated shoe box (see Plate 24), and viewed through one or more peepholes which were some-

25. *Vue d'optique: "La Galerie d'Eau,"* Versailles

times equipped with magnifying lenses. (Undoubtedly, peep shows were contrived and put together by the publishers, not sold to be cut out and set up at home as a hobby.)

In putting together a peep show, the prints of the series (consisting really of wings and backdrop with characters cleverly placed in them) were usually pasted at their side edges to heavy paper which was pleated in such a way as to open out or fold up and collapse like an accordion when not in use. However, the peep show at lower right in Plate 24 appears to be built like a deep shadow box, with the set of prints resting, at six levels, on narrow supports at each side of the box. It's tricky, too, in another respect: it's upended and equipped inside with reflectors, so that the viewer seems to be looking straight ahead in the normal way, not down, as would appear from the picture.

The illusions of distance in peep shows are quite extraordinary, even though, as in the case of "The Crystal Palace" (Sydenham, 1856), no more than two layers of prints may intervene between the front, or proscenium, with its peephole, and the backdrop. A peep show of *"L'Exposition Universelle à Paris, 1867"* has six or more and is probably a more typical example. Illusion of distances was still further built up by two means: first, each successive print in the set, from the proscenium to the backdrop, is made in diminishing scale; second, the wings of each set—hedges or trees or the walls of an interior—are brought closer and closer to the center as they recede to the backdrop.

Peep shows were lighted in different ways, occasionally by artificial light. But most of them were constructed to allow the light to filter in either from the top or the sides. One example showing an interior had the roof of its box lined with gold leaf, lending an effect of candle glow. This was enhanced by pinpricked candle "flames" in the chandeliers and wall sconces. Another peep show of a Florentine piazza in Renaissance days had little cutout windows, some backed with coarse gauze, others with colored translucent material to look like glass casements.

The French *vues d'optiques* were richly colored studies in perspective, mostly of grand vistas, such as *"La Galerie d'Eau"* in the gardens at Versailles (see Plate 25). The itinerant showman went about carrying a collection of these pictures in a big flat box. A mirror was arranged in the lid of the box so that when it was propped up the viewer saw the picture reflected. The tableau was also curved slightly in its background box to heighten still more the effect of distance. When you find these prints today, you will notice that the title of the scene at the top is printed backwards so that the mirror reflects it aright.

LORD BYRON'S SCREEN

An early and notable contribution to decoupage was Lord Byron's screen (see Plates 26 and 27), started in 1811 as a pastime, finished about 1814. This is a fourfold screen, six feet high, covered on one side with portraits and scenes of the boxing ring, on the other by the great and near great of the theater of the period.

Here is an example of the trend toward the personal, rather than the purely ornamental, in decoupage. Byron took for subject matter his own favorite entertainments: prize fighting and theater. The screen was made up of cutout prints and engravings from the books and periodicals of the day, resulting in a highly decorative documentary montage. This is in modern vein, the topical, the historical—and at times even the humorous—aspect of decoupage.

The romantic costumes, the legendary beauties and actors of Byron's youth paint the screen's theatrical front with splendid bravura. Fold 1 opens with two pictures of Shakespeare, at top left, beside one of his monuments at Stratford-on-Avon. Next to him is Garrick, with his Westminster Abbey monument immediately below. On the left, in half length, is Mrs. Margaret Woffington. Of all actresses, Byron reserved his greatest admiration for Mrs. Siddons, whose portrait as The Tragic Muse, by Sir Joshua Reynolds, is at the center of Fold 2. Edmund Kean, as Richard III, is the central figure on Fold 3.

On the fighting front of the screen, Panel 4, is Gentleman John Jackson, the English champion, who gave expert guidance to his friend Byron in putting his screen together. In Panel 1 is Jack Broughton, "the father of English boxing," champion for eighteen years; he framed the boxing rules in 1743 which remained in force until 1838. James Figg, friend of Hogarth, and Broughton's instructor, is shown in Fold 2. In Fold 3 are Tom Cribb and Molineux. Cribb was champion of England from 1811 to 1823; Molineux was a Negro pugilist from Virginia.

Under the hand and paste pot of its designer, the screen was in 1811 beginning to take on the semblance of its pictorial form, at 8 St. James' Street, where the poet Byron was to awake one day to find himself famous. He took the screen with him through various sojourns in the West End of London and, finally, in 1815—after his disastrous marriage—to Piccadilly Terrace. A year later it was delivered to a public auction in Pall Mall as "The property of a Nobleman about to leave England on a Tour," from which it was rescued by his friend and publisher, John Murray, and taken to its present home at 50 Albemarle Street.

THE ANTECEDENTS OF DECOUPAGE—IN CHINA

Looking far back, over centuries before printing or even paper came to Europe, paper existed in China. Paper cutouts known to have been made there in the twelfth century are still in existence. It still is a popular Chinese folk art which the children begin to practice early, and their fathers and grandfathers take pride in the family talent. One cutter from a northern province, Chang Yung-shou, whose great-

26. Lord Byron's screen — montage of personages of the theater

Courtesy John Murray Ltd., London (B.B.C. photograph)

27. Reverse side of Byron's screen — celebrities of the prize ring. Completed in 1814.

grandfather, great-aunt and father were famous for their cutouts, raises flowers, fish and chickens for the express purpose of having live models around him.

Cutouts, in the vast expanse of China, vary from province to province and everywhere take on strong local color. Using scissors or knives, Chinese peasants, both men and women, have made an art of cutting, executing intricate delicate patterns or strong motifs that suggest wood cuts, with greatest skill. They seem to have a fine inherent design sense. Subject matter is as broad as the land and includes silhouettes, geometric motifs, birds (see Color Plate 1), animals, fish, insects, vegetables, landscapes, homely scenes of life and work, folk tales and the traditional theater.

These cutouts are used to paste on windows, revolving paper lanterns, gift packages and other objects. They also serve as stencils (see Color Plate 2) for embroidering slippers, table linen or bedspreads. They come in monotone, or are cut from colored papers and often are tinted afterward in many different colors (see Color Plate 3).

CUTOUTS IN SIBERIA

Still earlier, perhaps two thousand years before the Chinese paper cutouts, and before the existence of paper, certain tribes in eastern Siberia buried their treasure at Pazyrik, now known as the Valley of the Frozen Tombs. Among these treasures of ivory, gold, wood, leather and textiles were found wool felt hangings, blankets, stockings, saddle covers and caparisons, elaborately decorated with appliquéd felt cutouts dyed red, green, black, blue and buff. These represented human figures, stylized animals, plant and flower designs, griffon and Phoenix (see Plate 28), similar in form and color to the well-known Sino-Eurasian "Animal Style."

Sometime in antiquity, not long after the burial of men, horses and treasure, robbers broke into the Pazyrik tombs taking precious metals and gems. After their departure, water rushed in and seeped down through the walls. During the long winter months of Arctic cold the moisture froze, turning the entire necropolis of twenty-five tombs into a vast deepfreeze of ancient art. It was preserved thus in an accidental glacier for more than two thousand years for twentieth-century archeologists to discover.

Writing about these nomads *c.* 450 B.C., Herodotus called them Scythians.

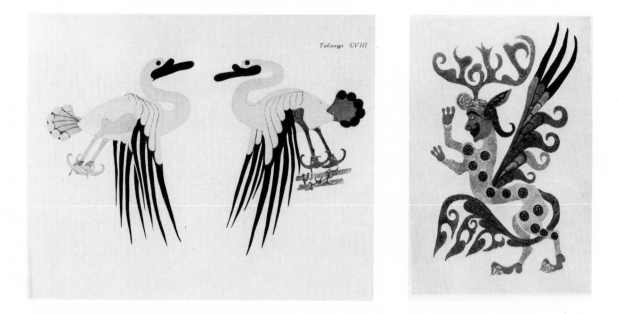

28. Felt cutouts from Pazyrik, Siberia. Drawings by John F. Haskins.

Whoever the ancient tribesmen were, their origins were linked with the fringes of the northern Chinese provinces. The Pazyrik knights, of mixed Europoid and Mongoloid race, with their high-bred horses, their excellent quality of wool and other rich possessions, may not even have inhabited the Siberian mountains. It is thought possible that the region was a sacred burial ground to which they transported their dead; it may have been the ancestral home of the tribe dating far back into the first millennium B.C. In any case, their cutouts indicate that their art forms had strong kinship with the Chinese.

POLISH CUTOUTS

In Poland, cutouts have been made by peasants for centuries; as a folk art it antedates paper. Like the Scythians, they used cloth, leather and also the bark of trees and sewed them on clothing for ornamentation. Later, after paper became available in the market towns and country fairs, young girls bought it eagerly, great sheets of glossy paper in wonderful colors.

Starting very young, girls and women developed great proficiency with cutouts. There seems to have been special wizardry in Polish fingers, taking the paper, folding it, not bothering ever to measure, and quickly turning out intricate, original

29. Gay colored paper cutouts
made by Polish peasants

Courtesy of Craft Horizons Magazine

motifs. They used knives sometimes, but mostly scissors — the great unwieldly sheep shears that were handy around the farmstead.

Traditionally these ornaments were cut in geometric designs — ritualistic and symbolic; in stylized birds, plants and flowers, or in small scenes (see Plate 29). They were pasted on ceiling beams, chests, bedsteads, cradles, wooden boxes and even the sides of stoves, giving the effect of gaily painted surfaces.

60

REVIVAL OF DECOUPAGE

Considering the history of cutouts, their antiquity and almost universal appeal, it is not surprising that, in one form or another, decoupage keeps on cropping up. The first revival of decoupage, as we know it, occurred in France and England in the early nineteenth century, when in England, especially, there developed a passion for decorating every square inch of every available object with something or other. There have been several revivals of decoupage in this country, notably the interest in it nourished by the late Caroline Duer, in New York, in the early decades of this century (see Plate 30).

More recently, during the autumn of 1957, an exhibition of decoupage was assembled in the Addison Gallery of American Art at Phillips Academy, Andover, Massachusetts. Tables, chairs, trays, screens, shadow boxes, lamps and even a baby grand piano were included, with at least one seventeenth-century Venetian cabinet. Entries in the exhibition reflected overwhelmingly the decoupage of eighteenth-century France, using prints of Pillement, Redouté and Boucher.

At the present time, decoupage is exciting enthusiasm within widespread groups here and there and threatens to displace the craze for mosaic that has swept across the land. It's a timely thing, just when in the world of interior decoration the cold and stark has vanished into outer darkness and there has arisen the yearning for rich, lush surface decoration.

Nor can decoupage be relegated to the class of "ladies' amusement" only. There is challenge here for the talented individual of either sex and any age who can neither paint nor draw; school children have demonstrated a notable talent for it.

It is said that in Mrs. Delany's London, not only she herself but others of her circle indulged in cut-paper activities. A little later, Beau Brummel took it up. There is Byron's screen, too. And it is said that the gentlemen of the French court found it a most entertaining pastime; nothing strange in that, any more than in their proclivity for tapestry-making; or in the sailor's enjoyment of knitting. Today some fine, professional work in decoupage is done by men. It is, in fact, a very personally rewarding project for anyone who wants to try it.

30. Chest and mirror lavishly ornamented, by Caroline Duer

CHAPTER 4

The Art of Decoupage — Composition and Arrangement

Before turning from the story of cutouts to their practical aspects — say, the kind of decorative work you yourself will be undertaking — it would be well for you to examine the principles of art and design that underlie even your smallest project.

Decoupage is the art of composition through arrangement; this is what gives any design its form. And since form — or shape, if you will — and the means of achieving form are the basis of all art, you will start from there.

Form, in its physical sense, is the shape of the object you are going to decorate. Within its limitations, your problem is to design still other forms that will conform with it.

Form, in art, has to do with style and period and is based on either traditional art, realistic art, or the purely intuitive art popular today.

In the world of fine art, the traditional form is painting in the manner of the great masters. Your sources will be traditional when you are designing a period piece, such as a Renaissance, Regency, Victorian or Early American composition.

Realistic art is the expression of the artist who paints faithfully an exact replica of a thing already in existence: "The peaches are so perfect you can pick them off the plate." Still-life oils are notable for this sort of thing. It is photographic, not creative and imaginative. *Trompe l'oeil* is the epitome of realistic art. It's a fun style, for when you look at a dresser so decorated, your eye suddenly catches a watch or a flower that is about to fall off the top. Now you are observing realistic art in decoupage. It's clever, it gives play to the sense of humor. It requires ingenuity and wit.

Intuitive creation in art, and in your workroom, is the spontaneous and imaginative use of the traditional and the realistic for the creation of new art forms. It is the basis of good design. Intuition is that sense within you that tells you when things are right and when they are wrong. Like all things in life it has two sides: positive and negative, conscious and unconscious. In its uncultivated state, intuition is unconscious. It is the wellspring in man that prompts all primitive art, is used unwittingly by children when they draw, paint or write. Unconscious intuition is born of emotion. But intuition that is trained to understand what it sees and to control what it does is the true handmaiden of the arts. One limits, the other unlocks. As you exercise the conscious, you become more discerning and selective. This makes for a fuller appreciation of everything around you.

Now, since all of us possess intuition, each one of us has the power to create. In art you let it guide you in the decisions you must make about placement and arrangement of your materials. It is that instinctive knowing when things balance, when colors are harmonious and your subject well co-ordinated through a proper selection of material. When you feel this taking place, and your eye travels over your work with pleasure, you are using your creative intuition.

BASIC FORMS—THINK ABOUT THEM

The basic forms in the world of design are the circle, the square and the rectangle. Within their boundaries are the triangle, oblong, half-circles, lesser circles, squares, rectangles and their many derivatives.

In decoupage — with which this book mainly deals — paper cutouts representing any object such as dresser, table, curtain or vase are based on these forms. Cut out in silhouette, a dresser or table is basically a rectangle. A vase may be a series of circles and oblongs. Curtains hung straight are rectangular or, if swagged, may be represented by arcs or part circles.

Starting with the circle and rectangle, you may find the following group of exercises illuminating. They will help you to think about and see shapes in their most fundamental aspect, and will give you a grasp of how to build a design from basic forms and how to place different materials where they belong within a given area.

Color Plate 1 Monochrome paper
cutout from modern Chinese book

Color Plate 3 Polychrome paper
cutout from modern Chinese book

Color Plate 2 Monochrome paper stencil
from modern Chinese book

Color Plate 4 Place mat by Loretta Howard

If the prospect bores you, try working these exercises with children — they will love them.

Using construction paper, cut out the following shapes in black and white. Do the same with a packet of assorted colors, but plan to start your exercise in black and white, perhaps adding a color later, and working up gradually to varicolored harmonies.

Large Basic Forms	*Small Basic Forms*
circle five inches in diameter	triangle three by three by
square five by five inches	three inches
rectangle five by eight inches	rectangle two by four inches
	oblong three by two inches; or three
	by one inches
	circle one inch in diameter
	square one by one inches

Using construction paper, cut yourself a basic rectangular area, say 8½ by 11 inches or larger. It's important, as you manipulate the forms, to consider the background you are filling as part of your problem, to develop a sense of distribution in relation to space.

Now start playing with these various shapes or forms, by placing the smaller ones within the larger ones. For instance, place the one-inch circle in the five-inch square. Move it around until its position pleases you, all the time thinking about what it suggests. A sun? A cat's face? A bowl for flowers? When you arrive at a decision about it, let it rest and pick up another shape, and so on down the line.

Don't hesitate to cut smaller or larger sizes. Try a few of the derivatives such as half-circles or odd-shaped triangles with unequal sides. You may come up with a good abstraction. Or you may get the beginnings of a Christmas tree with your triangles. Circles of different sizes and colors can be balloons; with bright strings attached, you will be leading into a story for the children of the balloon man at the fair.

Another simple exercise for developing a sense of line and its infinite possibilities is to play with a piece of white string on a background of black construction paper. This will give you added freedom and sureness in composition in outlining your future projects.

As you continue to manipulate forms in this way and work the simple exercises indicated, you begin to discover that basic forms are fun to play with. They may well prove to be an ever-ready device which you can continue to use many times in the future.

When the time comes to set up an actual design, to add the touch of realism, you will find your sense of placement has been sharpened and expanded.

DESIGN—WHAT IT IS AND HOW TO DO IT

When you get ready for a big date, a dinner party, or a shopping tour, you are actually a practicing designer. You make use of all the elements of design — form, color, balance, harmony and so on, and this very humdrum, practical exercise can stand you in good stead as a sort of blueprint for your art work.

When dressing, for example, you choose a color, a material and lines to play up the vertical and play down the bulges. You use a "focal piece of interest," say a handsome jewel of some sort, and place it artfully to attract the observer's eye. Knowing the power of contrast, you use it in your choice of color for your shoes, gloves and bag. You show a sense of balance and rhythm in the repetition of a touch of jewelry at your wrist and at your ear. You are, as a whole, a harmonious creation. If not, you rip it all off and start over again. In short, when you are properly dressed, you are a work of art, embodying all the elements of good design.

ELEMENTS OF GOOD DESIGN

The elements of good design, to give a rundown of the above, are: line, color, placement, focal point, contrast, harmony, balance, rhythm. All are important to a harmonious result in a piece of decoupage, as in any other composition.

Vital at the start is your intuitive sense of placement, guided by the planned relationship of the material you are using and the area you are decorating. For example, a scenic or an interior often tells a small story. The characters are given a dominant position and everything else is built around them. A flower arrangement grows as you work with it, again guided by your intuitive sense of placement. Flowers can be displayed in a free bouquet or contained in a vase of proper scale.

The focal point in your composition is that to which the eye is drawn. It may not always be the most important thing, but because it is lovely or arresting in color, or because it is in itself of exceptionally good design, it is put where it steals the show.

Contrast, in which color plays so important a role, gives your work drama and tension. Even when a composition is monochromatic (that is, in carefully graded tones of one color), it is the grading of values and their placement against each other that relieves what could be a monotonous treatment. In its simplest form, contrast is dark against light, black against white, rough against smooth. Textures create contrast — velvet against burlap, say, or paper against leather; shape against shape, action against action — all create contrast.

Balance and rhythm are achieved through color placement as well as by physical placement of the elements of your design; they will have to do with the juxtaposition of size against size, shape to balance shape, the counterpoise of larger elements with smaller ones.

Harmony springs from a carefully planned piece of work composed in keeping with all the above elements. Materials with which you decorate an object are chosen for scale, and should carry with them a sense of "the fitness of things." This is no more than a happy combination of subject matter, color, texture and design.

TYPES OF DESIGN

Of the various types of design, three categories will be of paramount interest to you in planning your decoupage. These are the representational, geometric and abstract.

A representational design may be a fragment of life itself or any existing object: birds in flight, flying in formation, forming a pattern. It may be something static, as a ruin, or a seventeenth-century interior, a statue, a chair or a hitching post. Its aim is to represent a thing, objectively, to the beholder. The shadow box by Mrs. Hinchliffe is an example of representational design. (Plate 53.)

Abstract design is of something "abstracted" from nature, taken from but not literally representing a natural object. A painting of a tree, for example, may not look like a tree; it may be treated freely, stylized, suggesting a tree in form, line or

31

color. William Harris' collage, "Sandpipers on the Beach," is an abstract design. (See Plate 13.)

The geometric in its formal sense is related to the abstract. In fact, one refers to the designs in many old quilts as geometric abstractions. But in its pure sense, geometric design is a carefully worked out series of points and balances designed to fit the frontiers within which it is set. It is mathematical and precise in concept, and for this reason carries the burden of limitation. However, it has a place. In your work it may appear in certain forms of nature, as in flowers or shells; in architectural elements, such as an arch, a gateway or a tessellated floor.

YOUR ROLE IN DESIGNING

Having a set of mechanics is one thing. Interpreting and giving them life and glow is quite another. Here is where you apply your intuitive creativeness, your spontaneity, your taste, your feeling for what you are doing. Knowing when a composition has enough going on in it is like knowing, in a gathering of people, the right moment to rise and go home. Don't crowd your designs or they will look labored and heavy. Remember that air is around everything we do, that understatement is always the best rule. Good work shows this and gives the effect of being effortless.

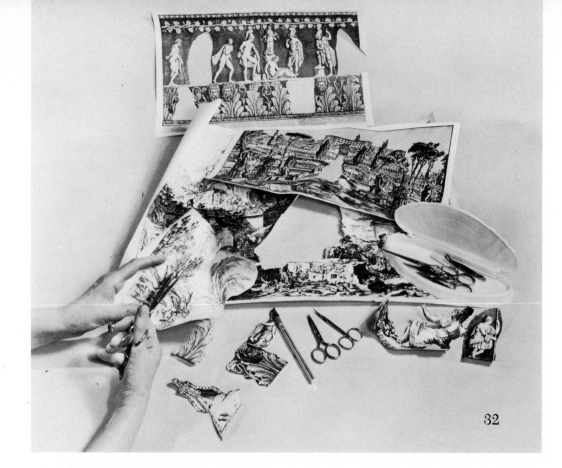

32

31. Three Piranesi prints to be cut out and redesigned for the tea chest in Plate 42. 32. Dorothy Harrower, having decided on elements to combine, as well as placement, shows how to use the scissors as she cuts them out. 33. Mrs. Harrower begins to paste them up with damp cloth in hand to smooth cutouts in place and clean their edges as she goes along.

33

HOW TO SET UP A DESIGN

When it comes to setting up a design, recall the workout of getting ready for a party. That analogy gives you a résumé of the elements of good design and how to apply them; a clue, perhaps, to the introduction of realism — a rose, a butterfly, a ruined temple. It holds for you, unobtrusively in the background, a framework on which to build your picture.

The first step, as a rule, for a professional piece of work is to rough in, on a piece of tracing paper, an outline of forms and their related placement. In this case it has been decided to decorate a door panel, one of a pair, with a floral motif. Make a rough sketch on a piece of tracing paper the exact size of one door panel, with circles indicating flowers of various sizes and oblongs outlining the leaves. Tape it along the top to hold it in place on your worktable.

The next step is to place your cutouts on the variously sized circles and your leaves and stems on the related oblong areas. Secure each cutout in its place with Stik-tacks — so you can lift a cutout for rearrangement as you build up your design.

When every piece has been placed to your satisfaction, lift the entire panel of tracing paper with the cutouts attached to it and hang it close to the object to be decorated.

Now start transferring it, piece by piece with its Stik-tack attached, to the spot on the panel exactly corresponding to the one it held on the tracing paper. When it all looks right to you as you stand off to scrutinize it, you are ready for pasting up. As you paste, remove each Stik-tack and replace it in its folder for use later.

You will discover that measuring distance and establishing an exact center when you are decorating two or more panels which are identical is important. In fact, no matter what you are decorating, measuring distance for placement is advisable. If you will examine the chest (Plate 44) decorated by Caroline Duer, you will observe how carefully each bouquet on the doors was measured and matched. The effect is as though two prints in reverse had been used, instead of two cutout arrangements re-designed from many infinitesimal bits of flower and bud and leaf. (The composition was restricted to cutouts from the wallpaper behind the chest; so, too, for the mirror.) Small pieces hardly require this elaborate routine for measuring and placing, but for screens, pictures, murals and all large pieces of furniture it is indispensable.

CHAPTER 5

Cutting Out and Pasting Up—How to Do Them

CUTTING OUT

In painting, the artist strives to merge the edges of an object with the background, so that they become one. In cutting prints the same idea obtains.

If you hold your scissors as you would when cutting a piece of cloth, the result will be a hard, raw edge showing the color of the underside of the print. But if you tilt or slant your scissors away from you and slightly toward the right, you will get soft beveled edges that are rounded toward the underside. This gives a most desirable three-dimensional illusion and at the same time conceals any color the paper may have on the reverse side.

Razor blades, X-acto knives, straight or curved scissors are all held in the same way. It may seem awkward to you at first, but practice will soon give you control over those beveled and slightly uneven edges much sought after in a finished piece of decoupage.

Some magazine articles about decoupage have played up the importance of the scissors themselves. These scissors, it is pretty safe to say, were important only to the person using them. The most intricate paper cutting imaginable done by Polish peasants was executed, as you will remember, with the heavy shears they used to shear their sheep. If a pair of scissors feels comfortable and you control it with ease, then it is right for you. It should have sufficient length to cut long flowing lines or short wavy ones, as required. But don't confine yourself to one or two pairs; collect scissors along with other materials and gadgets. As you pick up a pair for a special job, add it to your equipment and look for others. You will find before long that your virtuosity in cutting will increase noticeably and you will have acquired your special pets for the various kinds of intricate scissor work. Be sure to have one large pair for heavy duty, powerful enough to shear through cardboard.

When you have mastered the art of cutting the carved or beveled edge and are cutting freehand, you will notice a good deal of movement and interplay between your scissors hand and the hand holding the paper. This is as it should be, for it is this give-and-take guidance between hands that gives the feathery quality of foliage, shrubbery, bird's feathers and other delicate outlines.

You will find it necessary on occasion to redraw your subject as you cut. The arrangement you have planned will dictate the need for this. For instance, you may wish to fit part of a leaf against the contour of a flower. For this, simply place the flower on the leaf and draw the line you wish to cut. If you are good at cutting freehand, without drawing the line, so much the better. Otherwise cut your material just as it has been drawn by the artist to avoid awkward proportions and distorted lines.

In cutting large, important prints for screens, furniture, door panels, as well as certain areas in some smaller prints, you may find it best to use a blade for cutting rather than scissors. In this case, you lay the print flat and tape it to a cardboard backing so that it will not slip as you cut. It will be safer than cutting freehand, and the cardboard will keep the knife point from slipping. But of course you will lose some of the freedom of cutting in the hands and being able to move the print about freely. The cardboard that comes with the laundry package is good for this use; larger pieces can be bought from the art store.

If a print has a border with a great deal of fine, intricate cutting such as the fretwork of the three-panel screen (Plate 47), cut all these areas first. This leaves the outside edges firm and strengthens the design while you cut the rest of it. Next cut the inside outline of the border and finally the outside.

When you have cut out all of it, lay it between sheets of heavy paper to protect it and keep it flat. The large central subjects can now be cut freehand if you wish, or you may continue with them flat, as they are, on the cardboard. The three-panel screen illustrated later was cut this way, with an X-acto knife No. 11.

Working with very old prints it is often wise to mount them either on a piece of book linen or a thin piece of cardboard before cutting. Figures and even some shrubbery may have to be thus reinforced if they are to be used in a deep shadow box or peep show, where they will be standing, to a degree, on their own.

Prints on very thick paper can be thinned by peeling, after soaking in warm water, until you can separate the layers of paper. Work from the underside, gently peeling the paper off to the desired thickness. If it has become too thin when peeled, mount it on book linen before cutting.

If you are using old prints that have become foxed or water-stained, soak them in a solution of Clorox and water. Put the print in a basin or tub, cover it with cold water and add a scant teaspoonful of Clorox, leaving it to bleach overnight. This is only for black and white engravings—the bleach would remove all color from colored prints.

Do not discard the parts of a print you have cut out since these may be invaluable in building up some future design. File them away under their proper classification.

PASTING UP

As in other procedures to do with decoupage, pasting up is open to more than one approach; theory and practice vary from person to person. However, it is important to point out generally sound ways and means as well as the pitfalls for the novice to avoid.

It is further suggested that whatever specific measures you propose to adopt and whichever tools and materials you decide on, remember that today's industrial front is a rapidly changing one. Chemical formulas in the big companies are yearly, monthly subject to revision and improvement. You should keep yourself continuingly informed on new products and methods, remembering that even in the years since the war there has been notable progress in every phase of chemical research, including the field of adhesives. Even a world as small and remote as that of decoupage has benefited thereby.

It takes time for such knowledge to seep down from the great industrial laboratories to the small distributor. But it does in the end, translated in terms of quantities and end uses suitable even to your minor projects. So you will do well to keep up with new products and to try them out for your varying needs.

Some hardy souls used to make their own paste, while others used wallpaper paste, or fox paste as it is known in the trade. Fox paste is an excellent adhesive used, for example, on a sized paper surface, but useless on an oil-paint base. Many artists and artisans in the past have used lacquer as an adhesive, brushing it on the back of the cutout as well as on the surface to be protected. Undoubtedly, some still do. Theoretically, there's nothing wrong with it—provided the project also has a lacquer base—except that it's likely to peel and break away in time.

In order, therefore, to avoid trouble in pasting up decoupage, determine first the proper adhesive for your project in relation to the base you plan to paste it on and the protecting coat of varnish or lacquer you intend to use in case it needs one.

Latest advice from the experts is to use one of the modern water-soluble pastes or glues for best all-around results in pasting up decoupage. There are several of these on the market, such as Sobo and Elmer's Glue (see Sources of Supply). These and others of a similar character have the properly combined ingredients for gripping painted surfaces and others and will hold firm the work which has been so painstakingly cut out and redesigned.

These water-soluble pastes are milky in appearance, but dry clear. All of them probably have a polyvinyl acetate base which gives them a "bite" for sticking to any surface from paper to glass. They are used full strength except in the case of glass, where it is better to dilute them. (See Chapter 12, Decoupage on Glass.) Water-soluble pastes also are recommended for pasting cutouts on a lacquer base.

DuPont's Duco Cement is another adhesive that can be used for pasting decoupage on a lacquer base, but it tends to "lift" some colors as well as any gold that may have been laid into your decoupage, so be careful in applying it. Incidentally, the finishing coat of lacquer itself may absorb some of the color from your cutouts, especially the reds. (See Chapter 11 on Lacquer Finish.) Duco has other more general uses in decoupage. It is particularly adapted to gluing shell collages and the heavier objects incorporated in some montages.

Having decided which paste to use, you must next take into consideration the quality of paper of your cutouts. Seed catalogues, magazines and cheap prints on thin paper are apt to wrinkle badly when drying; and when varnished or lacquered, they sometimes do weird things, such as change color. This has, on occasion, turned into an artistic advantage, but there is no assurance that such will be the case. Should you be using such cutouts, it is wise to coat the underside with adhesium glue size. This gives a little body to the paper and prevents anything from showing through it.

Heavily coated, shiny surfaces like those of playing cards have been something of a problem in the past; their hard gloss prevented the paper from absorbing the glue or paste. For that reason it was always considered best to sand the underside so that the paste could get a grip on the paper. The development of the new water-soluble pastes has obviated this difficulty; about the only case now that calls for sanding is when edges must overlap and one of them is too thick.

The final cleanup is a thing to bear in mind even before you start pasting. Much difficulty and unnecessary work can come from the careless application of paste. When you are pasting on materials that cannot be wiped or cleaned (a paper lamp shade is a case in point), you are bound to have edges that will lift here and there after drying. This is not the fault of the paste. It is because of the extreme restraint you must exercise in the amount of adhesive you leave around the edges. This necessitates going over your work and applying minute quantities of paste with a toothpick or very fine brush. Lift the edges with your fingernail, apply the paste and press down firmly. Painted surfaces, glass and others which can be cleaned do not present this problem, and here you can be generous with your paste.

The best way to start pasting is to lay your work face down on your piece of working glass. Lightly dip your brush in water, then in the paste and brush it on smoothly, working from the center to the edges. Leaving enough paste along the edges is most important; you must be the judge of that. Alternating water and paste gives you an even consistency.

Another method of applying paste to a cutout is to spread the paste out on your working glass or a wide saucer for smaller pieces and lightly draw the back of the cutout across it. Working this way, without the brush, will speed up your pasting job but calls for the skill acquired by practice. It is especially good for any long pieces you may have and for small cutouts. This method is, of course, only for such surfaces as can be cleaned, as explained above, since there is almost bound to be an excess of paste at the edges of the cutout as you press it into place.

For a really tiny object such as a seed pearl or a sequin, you may use your tweezers to pick it up, touch it to the surface of the paste, and set it in place in the decoupage or object you are decorating—an Easter egg, for instance. This is a quick, practical way for filling in sections with beads or sequins. (See Chapter 8 on Helen Watkins' church in Venice.)

It is a good idea, as you come to the last stage of pasting up, to use a roller for smoothing out your decoupage, whether you are working on large pieces or small. It distributes the paste evenly and helps prevent bubbles and wrinkles. Pressure with your damp cloth from time to time also is advisable, especially around the edges. When rolling or pressing, always work from the center toward the edge as before. If, in spite of all, a bubble does appear after your work has dried, make a small slit with your razor blade at its center and, with a toothpick, apply a small amount of paste under each side of the cut. Press firmly with a damp cloth until the edges stay flat.

Having done as much cleaning as possible as you went along, you will not find the final cleanup too arduous. This is accomplished with a damp cloth, handled carefully, in the spaces between your design. If there are stubborn areas in which paste is thick, or which have been left too long, wrap cotton around a toothpick, dip it in Renuzit, and wipe them very carefully. Make a last examination to be sure all the edges are stuck fast—and your work is ready for varnishing.

Part II

Projects in Decoupage

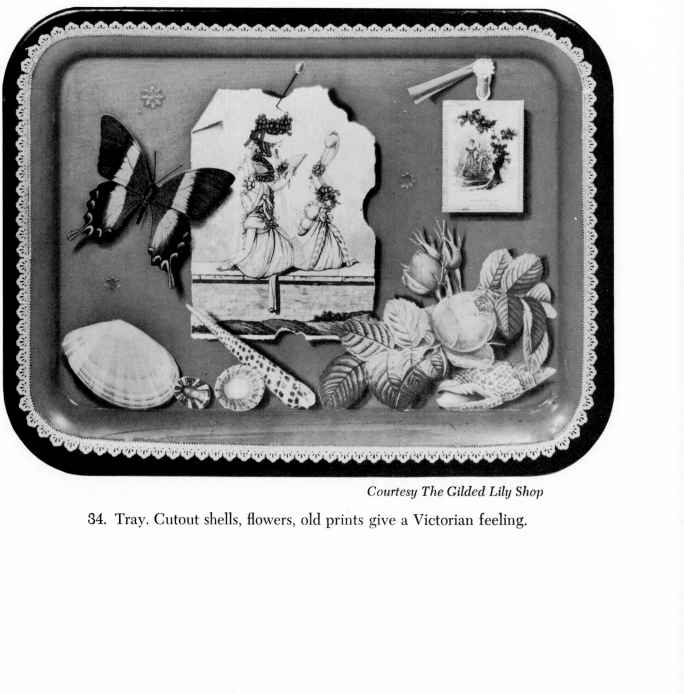

34. Tray. Cutout shells, flowers, old prints give a Victorian feeling.

CHAPTER 6

Trays, Boxes, Lamp Shades and Other Accessories

PROJECTS IN decoupage divide themselves, generally speaking, into two groups: the picture to hang on the wall — including collages, murals, *trompe l'oeil* "paintings" or abstractions, and shadow boxes; and the other, the useful objects to be decorated with decoupage—a tray, a box, a chest or cabinet, perhaps a screen under glass. There is a third category which might be called fun things: the purely ornamental, very personal conversation pieces such as a valentine or a memory book.

The examples of decoupage illustrating this section have been chosen to show you a series of projects that put into practice the principles of design discussed in Chapter 4, the suggested methods of cutting and pasting, Chapter 5, and of finishing, in Chapter 11. The important thing is to follow the steps necessary to build up a Christmas card, a paper-covered box, a lamp shade, a small chest of some kind and something under glass. For by the time you reach this sort of project, you should be able to handle an important piece of work.

Whatever you decide to make, the problems of design and of choosing the right materials will still be a challenge. And you will need to know the techniques and the proper application of methods. Make a study of the materials and surfaces you propose to work with, then turn to Part III, The Craft of Decoupage, and you will find set forth there the proper procedures to make your decoupage successful as well as fun in the doing.

You will notice as you progress through the section on projects that some things have been left to make their statement unvarnished; others take you through the number of coats of varnish or lacquer necessary for the integration and protection of your work. You discover that there is no fixed rule for finishing a piece of decoupage. The materials you use, the surface you work on—also the end use of the object itself —should determine the manner of pasting and finishing.

Paper surfaces, as a rule, as well as painted ones, can take a varnish finish, although this is not always necessary. Woodland arrangements, on the other hand, are best preserved under glass, as are other fragile subjects, especially if mounted on delicate fabrics like satin or velvet. The matte finish of a paper lamp shade, however, or of a Christmas card, is best left alone.

In the case of much-used household accessories, a hard-wearing surface is indicated, with a generous number of coats of varnish.

A case very much in point is the serving tray.

TRAYS

A tray decorated with decoupage can be a gay and intimate thing, or it can be handsome, formal, a period piece. Few things around the house lend themselves more to fantasy and fun. A hostess may like one for serving cool drinks or snacks, with mint sprigs scattered on a pale blue ground, a quarter of lemon, a slice of orange and an arrangement of glasses for form and pattern. Or she might prefer to portray her hobbies—music and sea shells. Where it is to be used will help suggest your collage story. If for a ski lodge, it could be filled with color and action; casual, personal in a summer retreat for two. For town the period piece, elegant and sophisticated— all according to the background it will live in. It needn't tell a story, of course, just be purely decorative, as the tray shown in Plate 34.

The tray illustrated is a happy compilation of cutouts that add up to a Victorian abstraction. It suggests a gracious, leisurely household. Through careful placement and selection the subjects have balance and scale as well as good color distribution. The butterfly is a deep tropical blue, the rose bright pink, taken from old color engravings. The colors of the shells are muted. The center print, with its torn edges, has purpose, for it establishes a feeling of age and gives the design a casual air. It is as though each piece when laid down had found its right place and remained there. The open spaces are restful, an element of the design, edged around with the

Color Plate 5 Cabinet in *découpage chinois* by Lovina Kenyon

Color Plate 6 Dining table top by Loretta Howard

Color Plate 7 Chest with decoupage of shell cutouts by Loretta Howard

Color Plate 8 Chest from Victorian England. Property of Loretta Howard.

gold paper lace and spotted here and there with stars for textural interest. As a finishing touch, shadows were brushed on in oil to deepen perspective and emphasize its three-dimensional effect. A deep brown tone, slightly grayed, keeps the effect soft and subtle. Always paint shadows as they would naturally fall from a given source of light. Some artists in decoupage feel that a piece is unfinished without proper shadows.

When you have settled on the subject matter for your tray, the next move is to decide on an allover color scheme. Then you assemble the materials to cut out, to arrange and rearrange, to bring life finally to the vision in your mind's eye.

A metal tray gets a preliminary coat of aluminum paint before the first base coat of oil paint. Otherwise the preparation of metal and wood trays is the same. After the three final base coats of paint, the tray is ready for pasting on your decoupage arrangement. For the preparation of the base, and the finishing and protecting coats of varnish, see Chapter 11.

The tray in Plate 34 has a two-tone paint base: the rim and underside in black, the center a soft moss green, three coats of each. For finishing, it was given eight or ten coats of varnish. The next to the last coat was of glossy varnish, the final coat flat, with the appropriate rubbing down after each.

In the case of trays—which take a beating—it is suggested that the routine on painting and finishing be followed scrupulously. Trays very often are subjected to heavy duty; they are set down almost anywhere, sometimes scrubbed and stacked in a hurry. The full twenty-four-hour period for drying should be allowed between each base coat, the pasting on of decoupage, and each finishing coat. The same for sandpapering or emery cloth rubdowns. Dust-free precaution also is important. (See Chapter 11.)

If your tray project embraces the plan of doing over an old tray, whether of metal or wood, see Chapter 12 on Renovating Surfaces for Decoupage.

To re-create in decoupage, for the owner, a country house or a well-loved garden is a specialty of Lucy Herndon Crockett. Her clever reconstruction on the tray shown in Plate 35 is all the more desirable for being personal. The Winthrop Aldrich house in Maine is a striking example of her ability to bring a scene to life, to bring out perspective, building layer on layer from the back to the foreground.

Miss Crockett prefers lacquer to varnish, both as a base and a finish.

35. Tray by Lucy Crockett. The Winthrop Aldrich house in Maine.

36. "Undersea Witchery," a tray by Lucy Crockett

This is one of those deviations from the average procedure that indicates the flexibility of materials and methods in decoupage work. She buys her trays already painted a flat black. Working from this base, she sprays it with many thin coats of lacquer before pasting on the cutouts so as to be sure of a firm base for the many heavy coats of brushing lacquer she applies afterwards. Sometimes she brushes on as many as fifteen finishing coats, cutting the last several coats with a flattening base to give it a dull, hand-rubbed look.

Plate 36 shows a tray called "Undersea Witchery" with corals, mermaid and sea creatures cut from magazine advertisements. The diver was cut out of a post card from the American Museum of Natural History.

BOXES

Boxes are useful things. They also are intriguing, so much so that they readily become collectors' items. And they invite decoration. In all their various sizes and guises they rest on our tables and shelves adding their bright share of good looks and usefulness in a hundred ways. We have everything from cigarette and matchboxes, to jewel boxes, sewing boxes, and right up to trunk-size boxes adorned in manifold ways. They are a natural for decoupage.

Box surfaces run the gamut of materials: paper, metal, plastic, leather, alabaster, tortoise shell and wood.

Perhaps you might like to begin by decorating a wooden cigarette box with decoupage. The first step in preparing a wooden box is to sand it thoroughly, inside and out, to remove any roughnesses and all traces of glue along the joints. After it has been sanded with fine sandpaper, apply a light coat of shellac or varnish and allow it to dry for twenty-four hours. Sandpaper it again, and if you are working with a porous wood, give it a coat of wood filler. After another twenty-four hours rub it down again, rubbing against the grain.

Next, apply whatever color of wood stain you want, or give it its first coat of paint. Two coats and sometimes three are advisable. It is important to let it dry thoroughly between each coat, and rub it down before the next. (See Chapter 11.) After the last coat of paint, a dampened emery cloth will give a fine, soft matte finish, for that well-integrated finish that is so desirable.

The surfaces are now ready for your decoupage decoration. When you have finished applying this (see Chapter 5 on Pasting Up), go over all surfaces with a clean damp rag, removing every bit of paste around the design or edges of the box, and begin your varnishing.

Make a small puddle of varnish at the center top of your box and spread it out from there to the edges and down the sides. Anywhere from six to ten coats of one of the new fast-drying varnishes will give it the look you are after, with light rub-downs between. (Try a dull-drying varnish for the soft rubbed look.) And be sure to give your box the dust-free drying periods.

COVERING A BOX

Assume that, instead of painting, you wish to cover a box with fabric or paper. You have chosen a cedar box with self-lining and a lid that fits over the lip formed by the lining, as shown by the cigarette boxes covered with malachite and marbled papers in Plate 37.

As in painting a box, your first step is to sand a box inside and out to remove any roughness and all trace of glue from the sides and joints. In doing this you should remove the self-lining and leave it out until you have finished covering the box. The lining consists of four thin pieces of wood, two sides and two ends, mitered at the corners so that they can easily be slipped out but also fitted back in together snugly. It is unnecessary to line or treat the cedar lining of the box in any way, even with a coat of paint. On the other hand, you may wish to decorate the inside of the lid. The inside of the lid of one of the boxes shown in Plate 37 was given a coat of flat black paint as a base for gold trim put on later. If you paste a paper or fabric lining in the lid, you will not be able to slip it back over the lip formed by the lining of the box.

Putting aside the lid for the moment and starting with the lower part of the box, cut a strip of paper long enough to run around all four sides and wide enough so that you can turn it under at the bottom, and over the top edge to meet the lining.

Begin pasting this length of paper at one corner, first applying paste to the side of the box. (Don't paste down the top or bottom edges of the paper strip

37. Cigarette and matchbox sets covered with marbled and malachite papers
by Elsa Noble

38. Round dress box by Dorothy Harrower and Helen Hinchliffe

until the sides are in position.) When you get back to the corner where you started, give the paper or fabric an extra dab of paste and pinch the two ends together. Press them down on the box for a clean-cut corner. When fairly dry, cut the material very close to the box so that you have a finished corner without any underfold of the material showing as a bump. Next, paste down the edges along the bottom of the box, mitering the corners. (Mitering means snipping out the extra piece made by folding at the corner.) In the same way, paste down the edges at the top of the box, to meet the lining, again mitering the corners and cutting off flush any surplus at this point with a sharp razor blade.

To cover the top or lid of the box, cut a rectangle of the material so that it extends well over the sides and edges, for you must finish them as you did for the lower section. Spread the paste on top of the lid and place the material so that it is evenly distributed on all four sides. Start pressing it into place by rubbing from the center to the sides all around. When it is fairly dry, work the sides and ends into position. Paste each corner and pinch it as you did the bottom corners. Let it dry a bit before cutting off sharply as described above for professional-looking corners. Finish the edges in the same way as for the bottom, cutting off any leftover material along the inside of the edge with a sharp razor.

When it is quite dry, put the strips of cedar lining back into position, and your box is ready to add any decoration you choose. The box in Plate 37 which was covered with marbled paper had a piece of black paper pasted on the bottom—to match the coat of paint on the inside of the lid—showing an edge of the marbled paper about one-sixteenth of an inch wide. Then a gold paper border was pasted around the lower edge of the box, around the bottom edge of the lid, and a gold rosette medallion was pasted in the center of the inside of the lid, as shown in the inverted lid of the other box.

To hinge a box, if you prefer it that way, is a simple matter, and it is then covered in the same way as the box with the separate lid. Set the hinges against the back of the box where you want them and with a pencil mark each side of each hinge on the box and on the lid. Recheck for perfect alignment.

If you wish the hinges to be countersunk or flush with the surface of box and lid, take a sharp knife and whittle out the rectangles between the hinge marks. A good way to attach the hinges firmly—and before you drive home nails or screws—is to give the inside of the hinges a coat of Duco cement before setting them into their grooves. This should be done in two stages: first apply the bottom halves of the hinges to the box, and when the cement has set, hammer the nails in; next, repeat the same routine with the lid.

If the nails come through on the inside, well and good. Just press the points down and back into the wood for extra security and tackle the job of covering the box.

THE ROUND BOX

And now for the round box, a shape that is perhaps more interesting and certainly more challenging for a decoupage arrangement than the rectangular forms. The dress box, shown in Plate 38, is bright red in color. Its shape suggests the direction the design should take, as well as the subject matter. It became a workout in designing a circle within a circle. The color suggested a Spanish arena and eventually, when a folio of bullfight prints turned up, they were carefully cut apart, with beveled edges as far as possible for three-dimensional effect. (See Chapter 5 on Cutting Out.) Clever arrangement of the various positions tells the story of the national sport on a sunny afternoon in Spain. The bullfight made it decidedly an action piece.

The box required no preparation, since the paper, with its shiny surface, was in perfect condition. It was the arrangement of the design that took thought, for the grandstand had to be built up and rearranged to make it fit the half-circle it rests within. This, too, had to be the focal point of perspective needed to suggest space and distance.

While the prints were all of the same thickness, the post cards used for the lower section were thicker. These also had to be used to extend the grandstand and finish off its end sections. Superimposing them on the prints raised their edges so much that all these additional pieces had to be sanded and, in some cases, a layer of the underside lifted. Other than that, the cutouts had no help. Small scraps of the earth were cut out also and set around the various scenes of action as a foundation for fast footwork; they gave weight and cohesion to the composition as a whole.

The small vignetted groups placed at intervals around the lower section of the box were cutouts from a set of colored post cards. They, too, depict the various positions of the bullfighter. The rest of the ornamentation, set between these and around the rim and top edge of the lid, was cut from wide, gold paper border. Eight coats of clear varnish were applied over all to insure full protection.

COVERING A ROUND BOX

Covering a round box is as simple, if not simpler, than covering a square one. A small jewel-case size, a bandbox, or a large hatbox of any kind will do nicely. Covering hatboxes is, in fact, an old American custom. Covering and lining them and lining trunks with wallpaper was a practice that flourished in early colonial days and through the 1880's.

Select a decorative paper and cut it the width of the lower section of the box and long enough to go right around it with a slight overlap. If you are using fabric instead of paper, it should be cut on the bias. Cut generously enough so that you will be able to turn material in at the top and bottom.

When you have completed pasting this on (see Chapter 5 on Pasting Up), cut a circular piece the size of the circumference of the box from another paper preferably—perhaps a solid color of lesser quality—and paste it on the bottom of the box. The lid is handled in the same way. If you are using a solid color paper, your box is now ready for pasting on any decoupage design you like.

Don't neglect the fun of decorating the inside of the lid. It is always a pleasant thing to open a box for the surprise on the inside. Add at least seven or eight coats of varnish for protection of your box, even if you have not decorated the outside with decoupage.

WASTEBASKETS

Covering a wastebasket of wood or heavy cardboard follows very much the same procedures as covering the lower part of a rectangular box. The wastebasket shown (Plate 40) is of cardboard with a shadow-box front, which will be considered as a separate project in Chapter 8. This basket was covered after the shadow box was completed and had been glued into place, glass front and all.

39. Box covered with old Chinese
papers by Lovina Kenyon

40. Wastebasket

41. Lamp shade decorated with cutouts by Helen Hinchliffe

Since the shadow box forms the fourth side of the basket, it was necessary to cut the paper only large enough to go around three sides, extending far enough on two sides to cover the sides of the shadow box. But first it was painted a light cocoa-brown with a flat paint, inside and out, including the bottom.

A rich tortoise-shell paper with metallic glints was chosen. This was cut wide enough to allow for a generous turning in at the top, about two inches. The corners were mitered, pasted down and edged with narrow gold paper edging where the paper met the painted inside of the basket.

The paper on the sides was cut flush with the bottom of the basket, not turned under. Then each side was edged, panelwise, with the gold paper trim. Two sides were decorated further, as shown in the picture, with the gold edging forming a smaller rectangle with crisscross trim and a gold medallion in the center. Into the gold medallions were set real cameos, three-dimensional like the one pasted into the lintel near the top of the shadow box.

LAMP SHADES

The subject matter for the lamp shade (Plate 41) was cut from a collection of eighteenth-century fashion prints. Of the three groups of figures, animals and foliage, each one required a very considerable build-up. Several prints were used for the purpose. The placement of the dogs between the figures and foliage acts as a tie to hold the whole arrangement together. Each print was chosen to blend with the others, since the delicate coloring of the costumes and foliage must be related.

The problem in decorating this lamp shade was twofold—first the matter of intricate cutting, then the business of pasting on a paper surface which permits of no final cleanup.

For cutting out the back and seat of the wrought-iron bench and the spaces showing through the foliage, each print was taped flat on a piece of cardboard slightly larger than itself. (See Chapter 5 on Cutting Out.) An X-acto knife was used for this fine, intricate cutting.

For the rest, scissors were used, working freely with both hands. The edges or outside of the trees, their trunks and branches were then carefully cut with quick, irregular movement against the slanted scissors, bringing to life the feathery quality of the trees and shrubs.

There is an alternative to this fine inside and outline cutting for those whose eyesight can't take the strain or whose cutting skill is not up to it. It is quite permissible to paint in these spaces to match the background. Taking care to get an exact match, you may use either oil or water color, depending upon the surface you are working on. At a short distance the effect is good, although it will never have quite the light and airy appearance of cutouts.

The cutouts were pasted onto an ordinary off-white paper lamp shade. This is a surface which does not allow for cleaning away the stains of surplus glue or paste. You must exercise such great restraint in the amount of paste you put on the backs of cutouts—especially at the edges—that you will inevitably find lifted edges after your paste-up job has dried. This must be dealt with by pasting them down, one by one, applying small amounts of paste with a toothpick. (See Chapter 5.) As a finishing touch, gold paper border was pasted around the top and bottom of the lamp shade.

The matte finish of paper is often desirable, as in this shade which was left that way. It could have had a coat of clear varnish or lacquer for protection.

For a more enduring project, you may prefer to go to a professional lamp shade maker and have him cut you a pattern to your specification. He will give you an opaque paper which you can work on in the flat. When your paste-up is complete, he will set up your shade with the rings at top and bottom. The advantage of the opaque paper is that you can give your shade as many coats of varnish as you wish, for lasting wear, without fear of any streaking showing through when the light is lit.

PLACE MATS

Cutout flowers, leaves and tendrils decorate the place mats (Color Plate 4) by Loretta Howard, who has chosen tulips, morning-glories and others, with shades of pink and purple predominating on a creamy yellow background. Mrs. Howard makes her mats of thin cork, backed with a feltlike material. Many coats of clear lacquer provide a fine resistant surface without in any way dimming the rich, soft tones of flower and leaf.

CHAPTER 7

Decorating Furniture: Chests, Tables, Screens, etc.

TEA CHESTS

An old-time tin tea chest (Plate 42) is a pleasant project for anyone with a taste for doing decoupage. This one seemed to demand a black-and-white color scheme. Its slanted levels and straight lines, both vertical and horizontal, called for simple handling. Its age was no hindrance; it could perfectly well conform to another day, another scene, for there was nothing about it to get in the way. And so it was painted black, and reproductions of three Piranesi prints were chosen for cutting out. The prints depicted trees, classic figures, architecture with ruins, supplying a wealth of material for building up each decorated surface.

In preparing the chest for painting, the first step was to remove all the old paint, stripping it down to the tin itself. (See Chapter 12, on Renovating Surfaces.) Next the primer coat of aluminum paint was brushed on and allowed to dry for twenty-four hours, under the table with a sheet over it to protect it from dust.

Three coats of flat black paint were applied, with sanding and twenty-four-hour drying periods between each of them (see Chapter 11). The final coat was rubbed down with a damp emery cloth which gives any painted surface a wonderful mellow smoothness.

Next came the cutting of the prints. Main segments of the design were cut out first. The slanted front of the chest presented something of a problem in arrangement. If you will examine the chest (Plate 42), you will see that it has a drawer at the bottom from which the merchant scooped the tea for the customers.

92

42. Tea chest decorated by Dorothy Harrower and Helen Hinchliffe (see end of Chapter 4)

On the slanted section, there is a slotted device for a label to tell what kind of tea the chest held. Just above it is the ring that lifts the lid, where the tea was poured in when ready for shipment. This lid extends up to the flat top of the chest which is rather a narrow one. Now, all these various surfaces were disturbed whenever the lower drawer was pulled out or the lid lifted. Therefore it was thought best to decorate each section as a separate unit so that no break in an over-all design need ever occur.

Each of the large cutouts was tried out to see which of the main surfaces it was best suited to. Finally it was decided that the vertical front space should hold the great stairway leading to the arch that dominates it. This much of the design has story value, carrying one into another world. The sides and top pieces were composed to fit the areas they rest on. Trees and the balustrade of the stairway were added for a more finished and effective look to the whole composition.

The lower section was a natural border, inviting a running frieze of figures alternating with decorative devices.

When the paste-up was complete, it still lacked something to tie it together. Finally gold paper edging was applied all around just above the lower drawer. It proved to be the last, magic touch. From there on it was a simple matter to paste it along the two slot edges as well as around the bottom. All the edges of the decoupage were gone over carefully to make sure they had been firmly glued, and the entire surface of the chest was cleaned. (See Chapter 5, on Pasting Up.) A fine, hard-wearing finish was built up, with ten coats of varnish, as in the case of the tray, Plate 34.

IN THE TRADITIONAL MANNER

The mere mention of furniture decorated with decoupage evokes the memory of Caroline Duer, the queen of decoupage in this country. Her work is known for its elegance, its lavish beauty—always restrained by a most discriminating taste. Her mastery of intricate cutting was equaled only by the perfection of her finishing techniques. Miss Duer insisted that twenty to thirty coats of lacquer were necessary for that incomparable patina which gave her pieces the soft illusion of antiquity.

Miss Duer came of a distinguished New York family and was at one

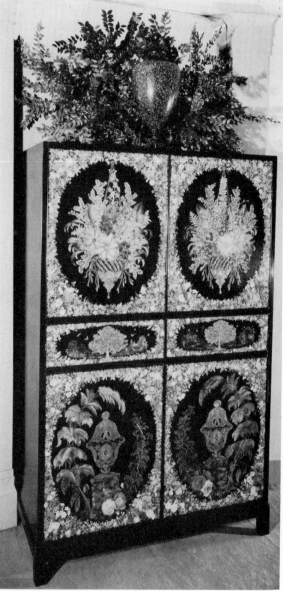

43. Cupboard decorated by Caroline Duer. Its doors are now at The Cooper Union Museum.

44. Chest and mirror decorated by Caroline Duer

time an editor of *Vogue*. She was a sister of Alice Duer Miller, the writer. During her later years she made a career of decoupage and drew great happiness and satisfaction from the classes she gave in the theory and practice of this graceful art.

A magnificent specimen from her talented hands is the cupboard (Plate 43), of which the doors are now at the Cooper Union Museum. This work shows her unerring sense of proportion and balance. The open treatment of urns and lacy fronds in the lower panels and of the containers above with their delicate burden of flowery forms and airy edges keeps the massive borders from seeming overcrowded and heavy. It is an example of opulence with restraint very much in the Duer tradition.

The chest and mirror (Plate 44) illustrate the triumph of art over limitation. As noted before, Miss Duer was asked to decorate these using no cutouts whatever, except from the nosegays of the wallpaper back of them. In less skilled hands this might have resulted in a fixed, heavy and altogether unsatisfactory piece of design. But Miss Duer was able to cast it in perfect proportion. The corners balance; the floral centers and the borders have importance with easy grace, mass without heaviness. Nothing is crowded; air and freedom prevail. So clever is her cutting and placement that the floral centers look like identical prints in reverse, rather than a paste-up of hundreds of tiny cutouts. If there is any quarrel with the arrangement, it is that the mirror is small in proportion to the chest. But even this was corrected to a degree by the solid massing of flowers and leaves to frame it, giving it the weight it otherwise would have lacked.

Miss Duer's work is difficult to emulate, not only because of her innate artistry, her love of luxuriant beauty coupled with knowledge of period; but also because of her infinite patience and skill in executing everything she undertook.

CHEST WITH CHINOISERIE DECOUPAGE

The handsome chest pictured in Plate 45 is the work of Helen Hinchliffe and typical of the elegance and delicate beauty of her decoupage. The chinoiserie motifs used on this chest were taken from Pillement prints, favorite subject matter of Mrs. Hinchliffe. In the redesigning of Pillement prints she has created a most distinctive style of her own and has used them for rich and well-balanced effects.

45. Chest decorated in chinoiserie cutouts by Helen Hinchliffe

Mrs. Hinchliffe, who was at one time a pupil of the late Caroline Duer, has remarkable cutting skill as well as impeccable taste. She also has a wide range of accomplishment in the field of decoupage.

Evidence of variety in the application of her talents is seen in the shadow box (Plate 53); in the lamp shade (Plate 41); and the Easter eggs (Plate 67). Mrs. Hinchliffe collaborated with the author in decorating the tea chest (Plate 42) and the round dress box (Plate 38).

DECOUPAGE CHINOIS

Using Chinese tea-chest papers to cover entire pieces of furniture, Lovina Kenyon has evolved a new genre, a unique and precious form of decoupage which she calls *"découpage chinois."* There is a wide variety of color and pattern in these papers—old patterns, gay colors that furnish richness of texture, give a feeling of great antiquity as interesting on modern pieces as on older furniture. As Mrs. Kenyon manipulates them, they sometimes give a Persian effect in the applied motifs, repeated, and the improvised borders and jewel-like colors used with silver and gold.

These Chinese papers, particularly the metal ones, have been used for wallpapers and ceilings in this country since the days of the clipper ships and the opening up of the China trade. They have also been used for gift wrappings, but only the metals are suitable for this, since the designs on the colored papers are hand-blocked on in gouache, and smear when they are handled.

For decoupage they present complex problems, especially on the scale practiced by Mrs. Kenyon. The paper itself is handmade and very thin, almost like tissue. It becomes very tender when wet with the glue needed to apply it. The technical difficulties in working with it, Mrs. Kenyon explains, are almost unimaginable. Perhaps the most exacting process is the fitting and cutting of each piece before the glue is applied. The paper can't be cut after it's wet; scissors or knife simply chew it up. And since the paper stretches after it's wet—and no two papers or even different sections of the same sheet expand at the same rate—calculating the exact size means constant experiment. Discouragements are encountered all along the way. For instance, the paper can't be smoothed on with too many strokes or it rubs right off the surface. And some of the colors are so fugitive that the lacquer applied at the end destroys the pattern. So experimentation with fixatives becomes necessary before the piece is lacquered.

But there are ways of rounding curves, of coaxing paper to follow carved motifs (compounded largely of patience and practice). And fragile as this surface seemed, it becomes as impervious to wear as any fine furniture after the layers upon layers of lacquer coatings have been applied. The play of light on these

46. Secretary with elaborate decoupage trim by Mary Smith

exotic surfaces is a delight. While these pieces are as durable, actually, as any chests or tables, they have the air of precious museum pieces.

Besides the cabinet, shown in Color Plate 5, Mrs. Kenyon has made desks, tables, chests and screens. The box shown in Plate 39 is another project to her liking.

SECRETARY WITH DECOUPAGE TRIM

A successful piece of decoration, combined with decoupage, is the secretary-bookcase, shown in Plate 46, designed and executed by Mary Smith. The interior is painted old Venetian red. This was the first coat for the whole piece. Then Mrs. Smith decided to paint the outside green as better suited to the *décor* of the room as a whole; when the desk and bookcase are closed, green is the only color that shows. Next she lined the inside of the bookcase doors with wallpaper in soft green, to match the outside, with a tiny Chinese gold pattern in it. She covered the two small doors at the center shelves of the bookcase with the same paper, and also the writing pad. The small doors, the pigeonholes and the little drawers below were all decorated with gold-embossed paper border, corners and medallions, giving them the look of old red leather books, gold-trimmed.

The whole piece, inside and out, was given a coat of glossy varnish first, then a coat of flat varnish. This was well rubbed down, given two coats of wax and a final rubbing. The chains which hold the front are covered with gold velvet ribbon, and little gold cords and tassels hang from the lower ends. Contrast, on the interior, of red paint and gold trim with the green and gold tea paper adds a vivid note to an effect of great elegance.

COFFEE TABLE WITH SHADOW BOX

Lucy Crockett has done a coffee table in black lacquer with Greek key border in gold. Miss Crockett lined the inside of the shadow box with black velvet and used it to display a delicate old lace fan.

It has already been noted that Miss Crockett usually tries to incorporate subject matter of particular interest to the individual for whom the piece is intended. The motifs for the decoupage decoration on her tables are small figures—horsemen, birds, butterflies—in various colors. Any colors will do, she says, as long as they're soft. The result is far from garish; between all those coats of lacquer they give the effect of inlay. Lacquer often tones down color, especially in the red range, making for a mellow, harmonious whole.

Many coats of black lacquer were sprayed on the table as a base for the decoupage. After the pasting of the decoupage was complete, Miss Crockett brushed on more lacquer, coat after coat. Sometimes she brushes on as many as fifteen. Just as for the tray (Plate 36), she mixed the last few coats with a flattening base, cutting the gloss, for a soft hand-rubbed look.

DECOUPAGE FOR A TABLE TOP

A special predilection for handsome old color prints of flowers, fruit and shells has led Loretta Howard to decorate her own furniture with decoupage. The fruit, flowers and leaves used for the table top (Color Plate 6) give an over-all effect of muted pastels, pasted on a soft cream-color base, making it possible to use the table with any change of color scheme in the dining room. The table has three leaves and can seat eight.

Mrs. Howard, who also paints, has special skill in cutting for three-dimensional effect and in placing long stems of flowers under leaves and other flowers to increase this look of growing things. Her work has continuity and style. The edges of the arrangement for the table were specially cut to give flow and natural line to the flower settings that seem to entwine each place. One of her sources for flowers and leaves in this composition was the folio of Dr. Thornton. (See chapter 10.)

CABINET WITH SHELL DECOUPAGE

Rare prints of shells in warm pinks and brownish tones on a puce background are another choice of Mrs. Howard's for a small cabinet which might have been an old music box, standing about thirty inches high. The top, which lifts up, and the sides are lavishly decorated. With smaller cutouts, she has trimmed the edges and legs of the table base it stands on. (See Color Plate 7.)

DECOUPAGE

SIDEBOARD-CABINET IN BLACK AND GOLDEN BROWN

Another cherished possession of Mrs. Howard's is a small sideboard-cabinet in decoupage with fabulous figures in a tawny golden brown on black lacquer. This was done, it is believed, in England, about 1851, but it looks more like Venice of the seventeenth century with its scrolls, its knights in armor, its legendary figures in a close allover pattern. It stands about forty inches high. (See Color Plate 8.)

A SCREEN ON GLASS

A screen decorated with decoupage under glass may seem to you an ambitious project, but carefully approached, step by step, you will find it not too difficult of accomplishment and you will be the owner of a durable and highly desirable treasure. For an exposition of the necessary procedures read the section on Decoupage on Glass in Chapter 12.

The three-panel screen shown in Plate 47 was done by the author, according to the methods described and in the following sequence:

The screen itself already had insets in each panel. The exact measurement of each inset was given to a glazier with instructions to cut glass panels to size and to bore holes in the corners of each one. The glazier suggested that glass one-eighth of an inch thick, the weight of windowpanes, would be safer to use than the one-sixteenth-inch weight, in order to insure against cracking at the corners during the boring.

Next the screen proper was given two coats of semigloss white paint, with the appropriate drying periods and rubdowns between. (See Chapter 11 on Painting.) After this a background of pale sea-green velvet was cut to fit and pasted into position in the panels. (See Chapter 12 on Choice of Backgrounds.)

The cutting out of the prints for the decoupage arrangement was now in order. The prints selected were enlargements in black and white of idealized concepts of a Roman emperor and his empress. Each print was taped for cutting to a piece of cardboard slightly larger than itself. (See Chapter 5 on Cutting Out.) The first cutting was of the delicate hatchwork scrolls and the inside lines of the borders. By cutting them in this order, the outside edges were kept under control so that they didn't

47. Three-panel screen by Dorothy Harrower

tear when they were cut out. When the borders and the bottom cartouche in each print were cut free, they were lifted carefully and placed between two sheets of brown paper to protect them. Next the figures were released and also placed between two sheets of heavy paper. Each print was handled in this way so that when the time came to redesign them, they were completely flexible, interchangeable, and none interfered with the others.

The design was set up on tracing paper, as described in Chapter 4. Finally the glass was cleaned and polished, and guidelines drawn to correspond with those on the tracing paper setup. (See Chapter 12, Decoupage on Glass.) The design was then transferred to the glass and pasted up as described in Chapter 12.

CHAPTER 8

Shadow Boxes, Murals, and Other Pictures to Hang on the Wall

A MASTER OF the shadow box, Carl Federer is equally adept with the decoupage picture to hang on the wall. His art is one of many faces, all equally sophisticated. His collage-montage (Plate 7), an abstract fantasy, is also a period documentary in painter's language. His *trompe l'oeil* shadow boxes are as famous as his Easter eggs (see Color Plate 15).

In the picture called "Niche and Corridor," a surrealist fantasy (see frontispiece), Mr. Federer shows imaginative handling of architectural elements, all basic forms cut from paper and built up realistically. Only the flowers overflowing at the top are cut from prints—paper-white narcissus, tawny orange and gold of tiger lily, foxglove, marigold and nasturtium; also the statue in the niche, the font and bird of paradise. Marble for arch and column is cut from paper made to simulate tree bark. Down the corridor, paved in orange and black with yellow walls, is open blue sky, in bright contrast to the mysterious blue-mauve night, lit through open doors by the eerie effulgence of a crescent moon.

Many of Carl Federer's pieces have story value. In Plate 48 a couple in the old-time South are seen courting. It is snowing outside; the boy has come in with snow on his boots and set his umbrella, dripping, against the wall. He has brought a bottle; but the girl is trying to persuade him to black coffee before he gets tipsy. The clothes, the furniture, the clock and pictures are all made up from paper; also that clever umbrella—which will never open or close. And the stove is a miracle of three-dimensional illusion. The only real objects are the lace curtains and curtain rod.

In the scene shown in Plate 49 the young lady of the house preparing to go out is all contrived from paper. In a French provincial setting she stands before a looking glass, holding a hand mirror above her head. The furniture and shutters are beautifully designed cutouts. Her ermine muff lies waiting on the chair. Meanwhile, the snow is caking down in the lower left-hand corner of each windowpane. It is all both realistic and evocative. Mr. Federer's sense of period is unerring, his approach that of a connoisseur and scholar. His lightest concept has literary undertones.

SEA-SHELL SHADOW BOXES

An enchanting and most decorative branch of collage and decoupage is in the arranging of sea shells. Their exquisite colorings and their fantastically beautiful shapes appeal to the artist as painter and as poet and philosopher. Shells are both jewel-like and flowerlike, lending themselves naturally to garden and flower still lifes.

In the composition called "Ornamental Garden Piece" (Color Plate 9) Louise Allderdice Travers shows a painter's concept of form and structure and an admirable use of color. Using shells in their natural colors only, she has gathered a collection from every strand, near and far, and has acquired for herself a palette of enviable breadth and subtlety. The nautilus, at center, is sawed in half to show his pearly, pink-shadowed chambers. The white, ridged angel wing or drill shell, holding the flowers, rests on a large pinkish-brown land snail. The butterflies are the fringed pearl oyster, pale blue and iridescent. The yellow, four-petaled flower is the baby foot, centered with striped tree snails. The white flowers are channeled clam and the lilylike paper fig shell. Running the gamut from palest pink to deep purple are the fan-shaped common scallop or pectens, the spiral spikes or worm shells, and the banded snails growing on the vines. At left on the marble pedestal lies the rare star snail, a deep mauve-pink. The arrangement is framed in an old gold-leafed frame, collector's item, about three inches deep, against a background of pale woodsy-green chiffon.

Although Mrs. Travers was a pupil of the late Caroline Duer—and has

48. "Courting Couple," shadow box by Carl Federer

49. Eighteenth-century French-provincial interior. Shadow box by Carl Federer.

done decoupage on furniture — she branched out early in her own direction, developing her own techniques for completely original shell compositions (see Plates 50 and 51). Frankly Victorian in concept, these arrangements do not smell of moth balls and the attic. They are composed with a freedom of manner wholly new, appealing, fresh— an art far removed from the heavy ornamental shellwork of eighteenth-century England, or the so-called sailors' valentines of the 1830's which were worked into solid mosaics in the octagonal ship's compass boxes.

Beyond the fascination of gathering shells, which obsesses her, Mrs. Travers also seeks out old gilt frames; their imperfections caused by age are merely an added charm. Her pictures are quite large, ranging in size from twelve by eighteen inches to thirty-six by forty-two inches. Backgrounds for her shell flowers are nearly always of pastel chiffons, although sometimes she uses velvet or satin and even linen. The stretching and pressing of these is tedious, but from there on apparently it's all pure joy. Mrs. Travers enjoys, also, the cutting out from prints of leaves, ferns and tendrils to combine with her shells.

The flower arrangement in Plate 52 is composed of the fanlike scallop and white cockles for the flowers, with tree snails at their centers. Repeated throughout for dark contrast is the shell called operculum, or the trap door the snail pulls in after him to retain moisture when he retreats into his house at low tide. The little spike snails are called horn shells. The butterfly is a pair of small angel wings; the container—a vase or basket—is the lion's paw; and at lower right is the rare star snail. One can easily see the skill with which Mrs. Travers juxtaposes colors, just as in tapestry where no blending is possible. She is able to bring out color values not observable in themselves, thereby intensifying the illusion of the breadth of her palette.

The shadow box attached to the front of the wastebasket (Plate 40) states neatly the impact of suggestion. Merest outlines tell the story of a guest, just arrived, greeted by his host in the foyer and ushered into the drawing room beyond. A telling economy of architectural detail—the pilasters and lintel and the dado—contrives a perspective far deeper than the actual two inches of the foyer. Well-placed shadows accentuate this depth, in addition to the fact that the chest and the figures of the men are padded out with bits of cotton to a slight convexity of contour.

50. The five shells of Anne Lindbergh's *Gift From the Sea.* Shadow-box arrangement by Louise Allderdice Travers.

51. Louise Allderdice Travers at work on a floral shell composition

52. Flower arrangement in shells on chiffon. Shadow box
by Louise Allderdice Travers.

A pleasant Greek-revival interior is built up with tasteful detail and colored in tones of brown, cream, gray and gold. Basic forms, as of the pilasters and lintel, were cut out of marbled paper which also covers ceiling and dado, creating intimacy. Marbled paper also was used for the three-dimensional, flat top of the chest which holds the golden lyre and decorated box. The chest itself was cut from wood-grained wallpaper (mounted on thin cardboard), as was the floor in a slightly different tone. Gold paper trim at the bases and capitals of the pilasters, edging the dado, lintel and other segments, also provides ormolu for the chest and decoration for the pictures on the wall. The cameo at the top of the lintel is a real one. The arch is set against the wall which is painted a flat, cocoa-brown, like the interior of the wastebasket itself.

The gentlemen are costumed in delicate pearl grays and darks, with slight padding set skillfully below the waistline, contributing measurably to the perspective of the shadow box as a whole, just as has the treatment of the chest.

The final step was to paste on the glass front, edge it with gold paper trim, and the shadow box was ready to be pasted to the wastebasket proper. Read in Chapter 12 the precautions necessary for a clean glass front. Smears on the underside cannot be corrected unless you pull the glass off and start afresh.

110

53. Shadow box by Helen Hinchliffe

In the shadow box by Helen Hinchliffe, showing a fountain and horseman in the foreground (Plate 53), depth has been achieved not only by the usual devices of the flat decoupage picture, but by building up actual different levels, using "ladders" such as are seen in pull-out valentines and in the nineteenth-century miniature theaters that flourished in France and England.

The scene itself required four prints, black-and-white engravings, all of which had architectural units and plenty of foliage. The background is a sky of silver metal paper, with clouds cut from the engravings and pasted on it in various related positions. The poplar trees, obelisk and some of the other foliage, and the great arch from which the equestrienne is seen emerging, were cut separately and set by means of ladders one-sixteenth of an inch in front of it. Projected upon this, and supported slightly forward of it by more ladders, are the "flats" of foliage, the steps and the stone archway at the extreme right, the lamppost and fence. The "props" are the fountain, the horseman, the nearby strollers and the shrubbery in the foreground. The "proscenium" is of plain beaded silver trim which edges the entire outside of the box.

Telling detail such as the box itself painted an elephant-gray, the silver sky, the piece of silver metal paper—cut and pasted on the pedestal of the fountain so that water seems to flow over it—all combine to give this rendering in black, white, gray and silver a special charm. The metal catches and reflects any color that comes near it.

For information on the construction of ladders for shadow boxes, see Chapter 12.

MURALS

The murals for the foyer of a New York apartment (Plates 54 and 55) are Rita Boley Bolaffio in her best *trompe l'oeil* vein. As if by magic, this decoupage mural doubles the size of the entrance. There is a chair on one side, covered with damask paper—nonexistent except on the wall. There is a deep niche, with a storybook Viennese ceramic stove in it. Using creamy-toned marbled paper to "build" the niche, Mrs. Bolaffio has taken a dark shade of the same for the column between the doors which is topped with a flower arrangement. The door trim, the picture on the wall, the sconce with lighted candles—all are contrived of paper. The only real things in the room are its four walls and floor, the two doors and the armchair.

Born in Trieste, Mrs. Bolaffio has lived many years in New York where she is best known for her dramatic window display. Her screens for windows and for interiors are famous for their incredible brilliance. Of all the artists working in decoupage none is more expert than Rita Bolaffio, none more versatile. Characteristically, she works in bold colors, cutting out flat basic forms, seldom using realistic elements cut out of prints, and yet building up perspective in her own knowing way. She accomplishes this through textural contrast, counterbalance of color values, and scale, often without recourse to shadows.

Typical of this technique is the picture, one of a series made for the St. Louis Centennial, depicting the Grand Opera House (Plate 56). This is a schematic, stylized concept of architecture which nevertheless comes alive. The artist has used nothing but pieces of paper, cut out and pasted and superimposed in such an

Color Plate 9   "Ornamental Garden Piece," in shells by Louise Allderdice Travers

Color Plate 10 San Gimignano, Italian hill town, by Helen Watkins

Color Plate 11 Orvieto, Italian hill town, by Helen Watkins

54. *Trompe l'oeil* decoupage mural
for foyer by Rita Boley Bolaffio

55. Opposite wall of *trompe l'oeil* mural
by Rita Boley Bolaffio

56. Grand Opera House, 42 inches by 30 inches, made for the St. Louis Centennial
by Rita Boley Bolaffio

57. "Letters," a poetic abstraction. Picture by Rita Boley Bolaffio.

order as to be convincing. It is night; the moon, the stars and the windows shine with the glitter of dark tinsel. The carriage is a masterly bit of oversimplification, suggesting the diamond horseshoe, the gala throng within.

Striking evidence of Mrs. Bolaffio's virtuosity can be seen in the collage called "Money" (Plate 18), a painter's abstract statement; in the *trompe l'oeil* screens; in the picture called "Letters" (Plate 57), an abstraction of a poetic nature, and in Chapter 9, a valentine, a Christmas card, a scrapbook. These reveal her variety of mood, the rare quality of her imagination.

Unique, perhaps, in the lively art of decoupage is the paneled wall decoration at Whitfield House in Barrytown, New York. This in a sense is the very essence of decoupage, since it reveals the personality of the artist and owner, his loves and his likes, the history of his house, a hint of the manners and customs of another generation as well as his own. James J. Whitfield, Jr., has given his work, beautiful in execution, a very personal charm.

A part of the bedroom is shown in Plate 58, showing one panel and half of another. Three walls are shown in close-up detail in plates 59, 60 and 61. All of it is put together in *trompe l'oeil* fashion. Each object in the various compositions is life-size and naturalistic in color and drawing. Mr. Whitfield got his three-dimensional effect by painting in shadows in water color. Every single thing is of paper; no object is real, not even the scissors hanging on the wall.

On the west wall a garland of sea shells repeats the line of the needle-point valance in the balancing panel. Crossed tapes hold an architectural print, an indenture document, a fan with *trompe l'oeil* engraving, Confederate money, a doll from China, a needlepoint pattern, a book and a feather. On the shelf sit an American carving, *Farmers' Almanac 1858*, a stereopticon, glass marbles, a photograph of Mr. Whitfield's mother, a porcelain saucer and some sheet music. Mr. Whitfield's signature is affixed to the ribbon-hung calling card.

On the east wall is a collection of butterflies and moths surrounding a bracket on which rest paraphernalia and books related to them. A matchbox hangs on the adjoining stile, and the key swings on the door trim.

A Regency hanging cabinet of matched-grain walnut paper on the north wall holds a collection of brilliant mineral specimens in addition to a Greek vase, a book on ornithology and an hourglass. Groups of old playing cards and minia-tures surround two drawings by Ingres. Wedgwood medallions hang from bright ribbons below the cabinet.

The walls of the room are papered in walnut-grained wallpaper in two shades, one of which Mr. Whitfield used to "build" his Regency wall cabinet. He also cut out wallpaper border which he pasted around all the panels in the room, including those decorated, over the windows and at the edge of the ceiling. Mr. Whitfield says that he applied no varnish or lacquer spray to his decoupage, and it has stood up well over a period of some years. This is in rather notable contrast to the practice of the late Caroline Duer from whom Mr. Whitfield took lessons. However, murals are not subjected to the same handling and pressures as furniture, which was Miss Duer's specialty.

In her series of Italian hill towns, Helen Watkins has devised murals,

58. Mural decoupage in bedroom of Whitfield House, Barrytown,
by James J. Whitfield, Jr.

59. Detail showing decoupage on same west wall

60. Detail of decoupage mural on the north wall

61. Detail of decoupage mural on the east wall

on coarsely woven natural linen gauze, in her own special vein, creating an illusion of old-world charm with a very modern polish. These murals are close to wall size, and have been widely admired as backgrounds in window displays.

Miss Watkins' particular forte lies in the imaginative use of the simplest materials for vividly spectacular effects. With colored paper, dyed paper lace, Pellon and Lurex she can re-create a medieval town, its sun-splashed turrets rising into a fabulous Italian sky and towering above dark mysterious alleys and broad courtyards. The depth of her perspectives is nothing short of magic, considering the simple, flat elements she conjures with. (See Color Plates 10 and 11.)

Several years ago Miss Watkins created something of a sensation in window display by adopting *pasta*—macaroni and spaghetti—as "drawing material," in a series of architectural compositions. Using it in its various sizes just as it comes from the box, she applied it with paste to dark net exactly in the manner of line drawings. One of the most effective of these is a replica of the church of Santa Maria della Salute in Venice, about five by three feet, framed in a deep shadow box of gold. The church, which is at the far end of the Grand Canal toward the Lido, is octagonal in shape with wide-spreading, angled steps leading down to the water. The steps are "drawn" in with spaghetti, as are the columns and the great dome, in proportionate sizes of the *pasta*. For curves, Miss Watkins breaks it into short lengths, down to one-eighth of an inch, and sets these end to end in curvilinear sweeps.

The medium is light and unearthly; its creamy color against midnight-blue net gives a marblelike effect. In order to give the composition the golden quality of a Venetian evening, the lines of the dome are backed with cross-hatched gold foil, the sort that comes in de luxe candy boxes. The small cupola above the dome is filled in with gold sequins, the spaces between the columns, with gold beads. Miss Watkins' research is done in a scholarly way; her observation of detail is as meticulous as her workmanship.

An appealing street scene in Italy, taken probably from one of the hill towns, is the subject for the shadow box (Color Plate 12) owned by Hope Williams of New York. It is thought to have been made in the nineteenth century, perhaps sometime before 1880. Although it has a depth of no more than three and one-half inches, it gives the illusion of great perspective. The house facing on the piazza, made of one-quarter-inch cardboard, or possibly a papier-mâché composition, is set in position against the background and slightly curved away from it. This increases the effect of distance and invites a long view down the narrow street at the left.

The walls of the buildings were roughened so that an effect of old plaster comes through the yellowed paint. Black window frames, doors and grillwork are slightly grayed with age. The tiny tiles of the roofs were precision-cut, laid in as though by a master artisan and given a dull coat of Venetian red. A slaglike material covers the foundation and merges with the rough paving. Small figures of an old man and woman face the piazza before their front door, establishing scale and adding a touch of intimacy.

FLOWER PICTURE IN PAPER LACE

The beveled edges of paper-lace doilies, as well as the many floral motifs in their design, make them an easy medium for decoupage. They need little cutting and take color beautifully if you simply dip them in whatever shade of dye you want.

The floral arrangement (Plate 62) required several doilies with flowers of different sizes, and one gold paper table mat. The vase was cut from gray construction paper scaled in size and shape for the nine- by twelve-inch blue paper mat it was to be mounted on. Light pencil strokes indicate the ridged form of the vase; more were added just above the foot of the vase for three-dimensional effect.

The first step was to paste the vase in position on the mat. Next, a large section of one doily, cut to look like a flower, was placed a little off-center of the vase, with parts of it overlapping the top. Then the golden tendrils were cut from the paper table mat and arranged in such a way that the entire shape of the composition could be worked out after gluing them into position. It was a simple matter to add the rest; a close examination with a magnifying glass would show how it all went together.

The trick in pasting flower arrangements is first to make your layout of the actual material so that you will have a pretty fair idea of what the various steps will be, and which comes after which. When you start pasting, use only a dab of paste

120

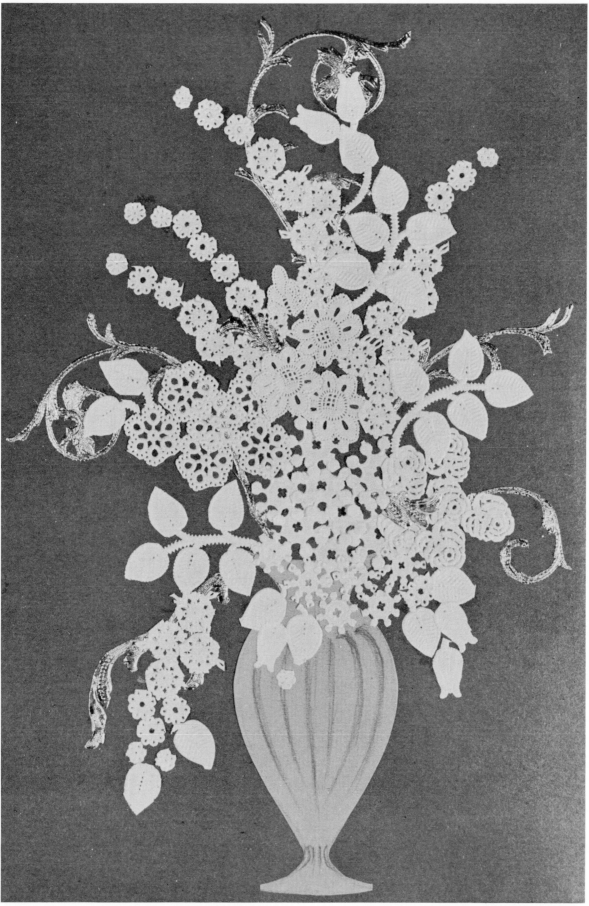

62. Paper-lace decoupage picture

63. Picture in woodland materials by Mary Brown Moon

at the center of each piece as you place it. This leaves the edges free for the many parts that go under, as well as over, in your design.

The object in all floral compositions is to keep them light, airy, alive. One should be able to go into the bouquet with the hand and rearrange it at will. Solid arrangements of flowers are as dull and heavy as a brick wall.

WOODLAND PICTURES

Delicate forms of fern frond and leaf, of small dried flowers and lichens have been chosen as background for fable and fairy-tale scenes by Mrs. Mary Brown Moon. Mrs. Moon combines the plant forms to make forest, foliage, meadow and swooping hawks, with tiny cutouts from old prints of shy woodland creatures—the hare, the field mouse, the baby deer. In Plate 63 a picture tells the story of a sleeping pussycat, dressed as a hunter. Reaching from behind him is a small rabbit locking Pussy's gun so it won't go off and shoot the little creatures playing in the meadow.

Each of Mrs. Moon's arrangements is a work of art small in scale and delicate in color, perfect to hang on the wall of a child's room. She has been particular about her selection of mounting paper which usually is fairly stiff and in soft off-beat earth colors. In Plate 64, the edges of the folded sides have been torn and painted with gold to give depth to this picture with its rocky boulders (fungus), its swaying

64. Composition in woodland materials by Mary Brown Moon

trees and its moment of gossip between bright-eyed mouse and bird. It is well to remember that children are adept at decoupage and that your child might as soon make one as look at one.

PINPRICK PICTURES

Pinprick pictures are of ancient origin. Earliest examples of them were made in China in the eighth century, it is said. They have been found in every European country from Russia to Spain, mainly of eighteenth- and early nineteenth-century dating. Nuns in a convent on the island of Malta, and Napoleonic prisoners in Dartmoor prison are supposed to have done them. Certainly it was considered an elegant accomplishment for young ladies of the Victorian era in England.

Pinpricking is a minor art that fits in neatly with decoupage, if not actually a branch of it. It adds depth, texture, emphasis of outline to painting or print and has been used to effect translucence. It is easy to practice, requiring more patience than art, although some of the early specimens, with their extraordinary complexity, belie the notion. Certain pictures have as many as eight or nine hundred tiny holes to the square inch in some areas, giving them an embossed, three-dimensional effect.

At least the equipment is simple, consisting of a small assortment of needles and pins. You may have ideas about making larger holes with a small awl, using a darning needle for medium holes. But a needle is best for very fine ones. Needles can be embedded in cork so they won't pierce your hand.

In pinpricking, the first step is to think carefully about what you wish to bring out in the picture, what you want it to say. The three old men in Plate 65, of French or Swiss early eighteenth-century origin, are a good example of the heavy pin-prick technique, the holes running like creases for the folds of their garments, with myriad fine ones to fill the spaces within, simulating the woven texture of cloth. Note the rhythmic flow of the lines and the interesting pattern they make.

Favorite subjects in England and France were eighteenth-century fashion prints — brides and elegant Watteau shepherdesses in color. These were further enhanced by pinpricking the embroideries and the laces of their costumes and head-dresses. Some of the early pricking was so exceedingly fine that the finished picture

65. Eighteenth-century pinprick picture

looked actually like lace more than paper—a reason they sometimes were called lace pictures.

There was a practice of mounting the pinpricked pictures on gold or colored foil before framing them. Men's figures in elaborate satin clothes with lace cuffs and fancy waistcoats were elaborated in this way. Oriental potentates with their rich jeweled robes and turbans were much sought after.

A rare example of pinpricking mounted on gold is to be seen in the print room of the Cooper Union Museum. This picture of the Virgin and Child was made in Russia in 1710 and was pricked in very fine outline on the thinnest of white paper. The gold comes through, shining faintly, for the halos and all. The delicacy of the white and pale gold lends the picture an indefinable religious aura, very beautiful indeed.

Pinpricking can be exceptionally effective in shadow boxes. Take a hand-colored engraving that pictures a street with fine houses along one side. Cut out the windowpanes, pinprick the outlines of the houses, the doors and the grillwork, perhaps, if any. Then frame the picture in a shadow box lighted from behind. The same device will work for an interior, pinpricking the candle "flames" in the chandeliers and wall sconces.

TINSEL PICTURES

During the early part of the nineteenth century, decorating prints of well-known actors, costumed for the romantic roles of Shakespeare's plays, was a popular pastime. These prints were cut out, pasted up with richly colored satins or brocades and garnished with bright metal foil, then framed and hung on the wall with pride.

These tinsel pictures were hand-colored in bright primary colors with a strange luster of their own, to this day a trade secret. With each print was sold a set of foil pieces, stamped out by machine to fit the various parts of the costume and its accessories. It required little skill to glue them in place.

The two prints (Plates 66 and 20) show tinsel pictures of Mr. Ellsgood and of Mr. Kemble, both Shakespearean actors of considerable repute. Mr. Ellsgood's costume was cut out at skirt, bodice and sleeve to be replaced by white satin. Tinsel

66. Nineteenth-century tinsel picture

cutouts were then pasted over the mailed fist with sword, the crown, the shield and the belt.

West's theatrical portrait of Mr. Kemble had relatively little tinsel trimming. Woven damask in rosy red replaced the long sheath that covers the figure. Bright-red satin was pasted on the headpiece and the mantle which was lined with white satin. The ermine tails were painted on. Royal-blue satin was pasted on for sleeves, with satin in deep beige for the gauntlet of the right hand. Tinsel adorned the band at the bottom of the skirt, the shoes, the sword hilt, the hand and cap, with the addition of real baguettes. It was not considered amiss to add jewels to these pictures, particularly when they portrayed women.

Today an even more glowing treatment has been devised for these prints when suitable ones can be found. Hand-colored, eighteenth-century fashion prints of both men and women are cut in outline as for decoupage. Razor-thin slits are made along the folds of the costumes and whisper-slight slivers of the paper cut away. Then the figure is mounted on a backing of colored metal foil which gleams through at these almost imperceptible "seams." The effect is richly flamboyant. Before it is framed, the figure can be given discreet padding, of either modeling clay or cotton wool, on the underside for pleasing contours. When ready they can be glued here and there along the edges of their respective backgrounds and framed. In a good light they take on depth and a wonderful glow.

MAGAZINE COVER IN DECOUPAGE

Decoupage has many and varied applications, as you have seen. An original and clever use of the medium—and one which belongs in the graphic or picture department—appears on the cover of *House Beautiful* magazine (Color Plate 13), designed and put together by Cecilia Staples, formerly of Staples and Smith.

This copy of the magazine obviously was a "family" issue, celebrating the joys of home with its legend: "Home Is Where The Heart Is." Decoupage furnishes the right touch of informality for the theme; reflects the feeling of young couples of taste and talent who like making decorative things themselves for their own houses.

Color Plate 12 Shadow-box picture of hill town in Italy, made in mid-ninteenth century. Property of Hope Williams.

Color Plate 13 A cover of *House Beautiful* magazine from decoupage by Cecilia Staples

Color Plate 14   Easter eggs by Carl Federer

Photo by Paula Morse

Color Plate 15   Valentine by Carl Federer

Photo by Paula Morse

CHAPTER 9

Easter Eggs, Valentines, Christmas Cards, Scrapbooks

THE DECORATION of eggs for the Eastertide festival is an ancient tradition throughout Christendom, especially in the countries of eastern Europe. Symbol of spring, fertility and new life, the egg became an object of fabulous ornamentation. Particularly this was true in the old Russia during the years when Fabergé, the French craftsman, decorated them for the czars. They were done in brilliant enamels, elaborately trimmed with gold and precious stones. Fabergé's trinkets gave impetus to the custom in this country where it has been taken up with sparkling results by artists in decoupage.

The eggs shown in Plate 67 were decorated by Helen Hinchliffe. They are made of opaque milk glass, unpainted. On this softly luminous surface Mrs. Hinchliffe has pasted scroll-like gold paper cutouts, lyre and flower motifs, and studded them with pearls, rhinestones and other gems. She has set in medallions edged with pearls or gold paper lace adding a warm, vibrant color note. These are set on small stands, some simple, some ornate, made from buttons of assorted sizes, then painted and set with pearls or rhinestones.

Carl Federer has many ways of decorating Easter eggs (see Color Plate 14). In true Fabergé tradition, many of them are lacquered in brilliant colors — turquoise, delphinium blue, shocking pink, purple — and decorated with bandings of

129

67. Easter eggs by Helen Hinchliffe

paper lace, gold or silver paper borders and ornaments, and narrow paper strips in contrasting colors. He uses a great many stones such as turquoise, amber, brilliants and pearls, and tiny beads in vivid hues. He pastes on small bright cutouts — a minute fan, a golden harp, a cherub head with wings. Sometimes he crowns the top with the smallest imaginable flowers, artificial rosebuds or violets. He likes to combine shocking pink with black, pale pink and white; or pale blue with deep violet, banded with cerise and gold. But his color story is an endless one, and ravishing.

Mr. Federer sets the decorated egg on a small cylindrical base made of wood, banded with gold or silver edging often contrasting with the scheme above it, then glues a circle of decorative paper on the bottom. The more massive eggs are set on colorful square blocks, sometimes rather simply decorated.

Eggs of milk glass seem to be the first choice for decoupage. But there are also ovoid shapes made of cardboard, and wooden forms are available or can be turned in any carpenter shop. There also are plastic forms which come apart around the middle. And there are real eggs, of course, those of hens and ducks the most usual.

These eggs are naturally more fragile than the artificial ones, yet when painted or lacquered have surprising strength. In Czechoslovakia, where Easter eggs are painted in allover patterns so stylized as to look stenciled, a method has been developed for curing eggs intact. However, the procedure in this country is to empty them. To prepare eggs for decoupage see Chapter 12.

VALENTINES AND CHRISTMAS CARDS

Perhaps you'd like to make a valentine for someone very special; or a card to evoke the memory of a Christmas long ago, skiing in the Laurentians, or cruising the Caribbean. Decoupage, in the simplest ways imaginable, offers you a chance to concoct original and enchanting effects. And more: you can make your Christmas card as personal as a pet name or a thumbprint.

Valentines and Christmas cards by Rita Bolaffio are designed and put together with the same verve and imagination as her screens or her murals. Her inventiveness in devising objects, backgrounds, and small props that heretofore have existed only in her mind's eye, never flags. Her themes can't be personal to you, but she can give you valuable pointers.

In the valentine shown in Plate 68 she has assembled all the suitably sentimental elements. A background of white, gold-dotted paper edged with a cutout flower border backs a cleverly contrived table laden down with flowers, also cut from prints. An old-fashioned gramophone is giving forth love lyrics in the visible form of valentines and hearts. Tied beneath with fluttering ribbons is a musical instrument for serenading, made up of small units of cutout papers. In working up her originals, Mrs. Bolaffio pastes them up on sizable backgrounds of heavy cardboard, two feet by three or even larger.

The Christmas card (Plate 69) has a black background with silvery-white snowflakes. The balloon from which the gay presents are streaming to the village below is made of strips cut from papers in turquoise, shocking pink and chartreuse. The Christmas angel is cut from a print; he wears wings of gold-embossed paper which also make the streamers and tassels. The multicolor packages are wrapped in plaids, stripes and star-strewn papers and tied with bright ribbons. The architectural elements in the row of buildings on the village street — façades, chimneys, dormer windows —

68. Valentine by Rita Boley Bolaffio

are contrived from paper cutouts with cutout borders from prints for trim. The little white church at the end of the street is virtually a Bolaffio signature. It is constructed with elementary simplicity in her most effective way. The door is edged with print and gold trim, the windows are cut from dark blue paper.

A dashing vintage motorcar sets the scene for Cupid in Carl Federer's valentine in pinks, blues and mauve (see Color Plate 15). The car is bedecked with forget-me-nots and pasted against the pink satin background of the shadow box. Paper lace and silver beading make the trim; note the paper lace hearts at the four corners. And don't miss the naughty glass leg perfume bottle.

132

69. Christmas card by Rita Boley Bolaffio

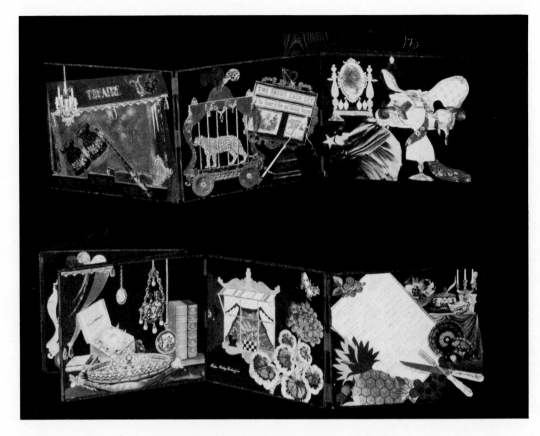

70. Scrapbook by Rita Boley Bolaffio

SCRAPBOOKS

The family album, the memory book, the scrapbook constitute without doubt one of the most venerable forms of decoupage, though countless generations have practiced it without calling it that. By whatever name, it is a natural for the most personal branch of decoupage.

The album in Plate 70 was put together for a friend by Rita Bolaffio who studied all of her friend's little manias and fads. She adored the theater, she was mad about exotic jewelry, she was crazy about the circus, and so on. The six-leaved folder was made of heavy cardboard, each leaf hinged on both sides with silk ribbon, backed with moiré silk and lined with black velvet. Mrs. Bolaffio has left out no detail to point up her friend's preferences for gourmet food, for wonderful clothes. She even thought to recall a trip to the Tyrol where her friend fell in love with the gaily decorated windows and their pots of bright geraniums.

134

Part III
The Craft of Decoupage—Materials and Methods

CHAPTER 10

Materials and Where to Find Them

Decoupage is a flexible art. It can say many things in many ways, with a limitless variety of materials. There are those who will tell you that you can use anything that comes to hand. And this is true, as you have seen in Chapter 2, The Fine Art of Collage and the ways of the painters with their *papiers collés*. It is true for you, too, since decoupage is essentially a personal art. In amassing your treasure trove it is for you to seize upon the bright ephemera of the passing days; not neglecting to hoard the small scraps of color — a newspaper clipping, a key, a bit of map or a bar of music. These are the very stuff of nostalgia. You may want to recapture a sparkling moment — a daughter's wedding, a day in the country, a voyage to far-off Bangkok. The more personal your shadow box or tray, the more fun to have it around, the more of a conversation piece it becomes.

There is no limit to the scope of your search. For a child's mural, barnyard animals are dearly loved, or kite-flying, or a trip to the circus. Men and boys like action subjects: sailboats or horses racing, "documentaries" of early motorcars, locomotives, or the trappings of their favorite sports.

As you work with and cut out different kinds of material, you will probably soon discover one particular subject you enjoy working with more than all others. It may be flowers, birds or Regency furniture. Whatever it is, you will find yourself especially at home with it. Perhaps it inspires and sharpens your sense of redesigning, gives you satisfaction and pleasure. When this happens it means that you are achieving a style. One of the great pleasures of decoupage is in coming up with a style. And even though you work with other subjects, you will find your happiest pieces are those done in your own style.

A most alluring aspect of decoupage is hunting for the right material to cut out and redesign. Your project usually sends you in search of prints, perhaps with something specific in mind, such as flowers, shells or fans. More often than not you come upon treasure when you are merely browsing or antiquing. Bookstores, thrift shops, auction sales, print shops, art-supply stores, or your own grandmother's attic — all hold adventure for you. The people who sell prints and engravings usually possess some bit of knowledge about them which they enjoy passing on; this adds zest to the pleasure of questing and kindles your enthusiasm.

Don't wait until you have a complete file of all sorts of prints before you start your first venture. Get together just enough material and let the rest follow. Collecting should be a leisurely pastime, yourself setting the pace. It can be an expensive hobby or it can be peppered with bargains.

Materials for building a subject are to be found in old chromolithographs, old engravings, books on botany, wallpapers, costume prints, old sheet music; chintz and other printed fabrics, paper lace, and colored foil; sea shells, pearls, fans; pressed flowers, ferns and mosses; feathers and coins. Or you may even run across illuminated pages from books rendered by monks back in the eleventh and twelfth centuries.

Such materials and many others are also in some cases subjects in themselves. And while they are given only as suggestions, they will lead you into exploring their sources. The following may help in that direction:

Chromolithographs are still in good supply today. They were the answer to popular demand for colored pictures in the nineteenth century. The better ones were printed in soft, rich colors on good quality paper. Cheaper ones were rendered, as they are today, in bright, raw color on thin paper. A good old chromo is considered a find and, while not expensive, is not really cheap. Depending on the subject and the artist, they cost anywhere from fifty cents to two dollars or more apiece. They are to be found in secondhand bookstores or print shops. The country antique dealer often has a few of them. Flowers are the best subject to look for.

Fine old engravings of the following:

Shells. Conchology by G. Perry, was published in London in 1811. One plate from this collection in color would give you a generous supply. To own the book would be an endless joy. Ask to see it at your library, and for anything else they may have in shells.

Costumes. Godey fashion plates are available both in books and sold separately; so are the Ackermann prints, strongly influenced by the French of the time; and for the Regency period you can get a book called *Corriere delle Dame,* published in France. Fashion prints of men and children of those days were not as frequently rendered as those of the ladies, therefore they are scarce and more expensive when you do come upon them. The *Gentlemen's Magazine,* published in 1828-36, has them.

Scenics. English country houses by Sandby is an excellent eighteenth-century source. Watts's *Seats of the Nobility, Carnival, c.* 1820, with many figures and gay scenery and *Vienna, c.* 1810, in brilliant color. Piranesi's *Views of Rome —* there is a popular edition of this that is quite good.

Flower Prints. Roses by Redouté, eighteenth-century French painter known as the "Raphael of flowers," are considered the most glorious roses ever painted. The originals are costly, but good reproductions are to be had for a fair price. *Temple of Flora,* by Dr. Robert John Thornton, is a folio of handsome renderings executed for Dr. Thornton by a number of artists. They are floral portraits, full size, set in natural habitats. Peter Casteel's *Twelve Months of the Flowers* and *Twelve Months of the Fruits* present elaborate arrangements of these in two folios. Paul Jerrard's little book of twelve plates, *The Floral Offering,* is another set of charming compositions of flowers and fruits.

Fruits. Good color prints of fruit to look for are Twining's, *c.* 1855; and a book of very fine plates called *Flore des Serres.* Weinmann, *c.* 1765, brought out a book of prints of which reproductions are available, in good original colors, of both fruits and vegetables.

Birds. Linnaeus' flower prints, 1797-1803, are shown with birds and trees; prints by Shaw & Nodder, 1789-1813, are small but in bright colors. Nozeman's bird prints, eighteenth-century, come in muted colors and are exceptionally fine. There are plenty of good contemporary bird prints to be found in books at reasonable prices as, for example, Audubon's birds with trees and flower backgrounds.

Magazines, both old and new, are excellent sources for cutout material, in color and in black and white. Copies of *Harper's Magazine* of around 1859 had very fine tropical foliage. Take note that one of the hardest things to find, either in black and white or color, is foliage; always buy it when you come across it. Other magazines rich in subject matter are *Antiques* and *The Antiquarian*. Try to find copies of the old *Connoisseur*, published in London, and of the French magazines, *Realités* and *L'Oeil*. The magazines concerned with interior decoration, such as *House & Garden* and *House Beautiful* are invaluable for cutting out. Others are *Gentry* and *American Heritage*.

Beware, however, of combining cutouts from current magazines with those from old engravings; the texture, printing and color of the different papers are not compatible. To do a well-co-ordinated job, you must be sure that the materials you use are of sympathetic and contemporary character. The glossy surfaces of magazine paper and seed catalogues, say, will accommodate themselves to each other, but are uncongenial with the old engravings and prints. Their differences cannot be reconciled no matter how many coats of varnish they get for the final finish.

Wallpapers. Sugden and Edmondson's *History of English Wallpapers, from 1509 to 1914,* with 190 illustrations, 70 color plates, provides an endless amount of material. Look for the old French wallpapers, too, and their Early American reproductions. Modern wallpapers also are rich territory; the documentaries of such houses as Schumacher, Cheney-Greeff, Katzenbach & Warren; scenics and panels from Louis Bowen or Van Luit; and from many other resources, florals, *trompe l'oeil* themes, copies of *toiles de Jouy* and others.

Fantastic decorative material for borders, figures in action, small scraps of scenery, bridges, swings and boats, of the same character, is to be found in the works of Jean Pillement, the Frenchman, known as one of the chief exponents of the chinoiserie period. With its decidedly Chinese flavor (see Plate 45), it lends itself to delicate areas you may need for such treatment, particularly on furniture, trays or screens. Watteau, the seventeenth-century French painter, although his genre was quite different from that of Pillement, provided figures and backgrounds of great elegance. Reproductions of his *fêtes champêtres*, especially, are rich in outdoor scenery.

A good many of the items suggested in this listing, as you no doubt are aware, cannot easily be purchased, since they will be found only in museums and libraries. Don't hesitate to ask for the collections of flower, shell, costume and animal prints, as well as the scenics of eighteenth-century Europe (Paris and Rome, in particular). Again, be on the lookout for foliage; you will find tropical foliage especially useful, with its flowing graceful forms. It will be well worth your while to do a little research in your vicinity for collections of books on the decorative arts. In New York, the Cooper Union Museum has one of the finest libraries of this kind in the country. When you plan to make tracings, take along a sheet of frosted Protectoid or Traceolene; it will protect the material you are copying from the pressure of the pencil as you take a permanent record for your files.

Decorative papers have a thousand uses in building up subjects for pictures and shadow boxes. Marbled papers made usually for end papers are perfect for architectural elements such as pillars, floors, outer walls and archways. There are dealers who specialize in patterned papers; also in solid colors as in construction and contact papers. If you wish for colors other than those in the shops, you can make them yourself. Take a sheet of good-quality drawing paper and secure it to a flat surface with masking tape. Apply the desired colors in bands across its surface. When dry, cut your color bands apart and store for future use. Japan paints are good for this purpose and will dry fast. Grays can be worked up from flat black by adding vellum white. These are important, as some of the most effective compositions are done in grays, black and white. For this reason, also, some of the old black-and-white engravings are most desirable, especially for pictures of shells, flowers and costumes. And you can tint them with water colors, if you wish. Dr. Martin's water colors, a little more expensive than some, are used by professionals and will withstand the rigors of pasting and finishing. These colors, by the way, are intense — one drop in water is sufficient. Be sure to test each brushful for value.

Fans and Fan Papers. A History of the Fan, by G. W. Rhead, published in London in 1910, has 127 illustrations, many in color. Dealers often have sheets of fan papers, in color. These show the fan spread out, full size, displaying the decoration on the face. Or you may have a cherished fan of your own tucked away, inherited perhaps from an aunt, beautiful in itself and something out of a glamorous family past.

Fabrics. Like wallpaper, printed fabrics lend themselves most favorably to decoupage. Woven materials stand up under a varnish or lacquer build-up as well as paper. It is interesting to know that when printed calico first was brought to England, it was used among other things to cover floors and given up to twelve coats of varnish to protect it. It wore very well, with a fresh coat or two of varnish each year. Decorator fabrics designed by such houses as Cheney-Greeff, Schumacher, Brunschwigg, Margaret Owen, Arthur Lee and others — sold in stores all over the country — come in documentaries, luscious fruit and flower designs, fascinating *trompe l'oeil* subjects, copies of old French *toiles,* all very colorful and suitable for cutouts.

Pellon is ideal for basic-form cutouts. It's a wonderful new material, used in dressmaking, with a feltlike surface but paper thin. It seems made to order for covering unpainted furniture, screens, wastebaskets, boxes and other useful objects. Its edges cut like paper without fraying, its decorator colors are a joy to work with. Also it comes very wide and gives generous coverage for the price.

Woodland material is a natural for both collage and decoupage. There are tremendous possibilities for small aesthetic masterpieces, as for screens, for pictures on the wall, for coffee-table tops under glass or laminated between plastic surfaces. Leaves, pressed flowers, ferns, grasses, mosses and berries all suggest a world of fantasy apart, an imagery with appeal for child and grownup alike. The forest is your happy hunting ground. A book press and time will do the rest. (The waiting period for pressing and drying is sometimes a matter of months. See Chapter 12.)

Gold paper trim — gold borders, bands, frames, corners and medallions are for trimming finished pieces. Ornaments include arrows, butterflies, lyres, coronets, cherubs and harps, of heavy embossed paper, imported. On boxes, lamp shades, wastebaskets, picture frames it adds that last crisp, professional touch. It also comes in alphabets, numerals — and keyholes — in strips and sheets, to be cut apart.

Paper lace is another bit of frosting for the cake, to be used imaginatively and with restraint. Like the gold paper trimming, it lends itself to edging wastebaskets, dressing tables, writing pads and a host of other objects, not forgetting the good old-fashioned valentine. Doilies come in many floral designs with leaves and curlicues all ready to be cut out. Paper lace is particularly adaptable to decoupage because its edges are beveled, giving the illusion of a third dimension. This can be increased as you become expert in the art of laying a flower, say, over a full leaf or long stem so as to raise it. If the composition is to be covered with glass, it is not necessary to paste down all the edges; an occasional loose edge adds to the natural effect.

142

While paper lace is at its most feminine in white, it also takes color beautifully. For this reason it can be used to good effect for decorating furniture painted in a delicate color. It can be dipped in a water-color solution or dye, then brushed here and there with a little gold powder for accent. A heavy coat of lacquer turns white paper lace to a very pleasing old ivory shade. If you decide upon a lacquer finish, be guided by the instructions on varnish and lacquer in Chapter 11.

Sea shells have always been prized in the decorative arts. They are a top favorite in the field of decoupage. Despite their ineffably lovely shapes and colorings, it takes skill and perception to use them well, and an eye practiced in scale, proportion and tonal value. Decorating with them is an art in itself.

Certain shells are used as flower petals, others as borders for picture frames and box tops. In putting them together you should have a knowledge of build-up that makes for depth and harmony. Shells have been used most effectively for floral arrangements, combined with cutout leaves and tendrils, mounted on chiffon or satin and framed; or for shadow boxes in underseascapes, most elegant for boudoir or salon. They can also be used for pictures, valentines, even coffee-table tops under glass. Mother-of-pearl, bright pebbles, pearls and other gems are not out of place in such compositions.

Lacquer or shellac enhances the natural surface of shells. They have been effectively used in compositions that were enameled all over in white or a pastel shade; even touched up a bit with colored nail polish. But this is heresy to some artists, gilding the lily with a vengeance.

Special adhesives are used for gluing shells, depending upon the amount of wear and tear the decorated object is likely to receive — a picture frame is handled less than a box. So, for the picture frame, Duco or any good commercial cement will do very well. A good water-soluble paste, such as Sobo, should be satisfactory for sticking light shells on box tops.

Shells are not difficult to come by, especially since shops that sell only shells have started cropping up in different places. There are many shell clubs, similar to the stamp exchanges for collectors. And there are the beaches where your friends and the bright-eyed children of the family can help you collect. Also, since shells always have been collected, you will often find them in antique shops and secondhand stores.

CHAPTER 11

The Workshop—Its Furniture and Files

Wʜᴇɴ ʏᴏᴜ set out to equip yourself for doing decoupage, don't make heavy work of it or be dismayed by the number of items you may need eventually. As someone has said: "All that's needed is a pair of eyes, a pair of scissors — both of them sharp — a pot of paste and a scrap of paper to get on with. . . ." This is understatement, of course, but it's not far off the truth, depending on the nature of your project. If you're planning a Christmas card, a small personal collage to commemorate an occasion, what the well-furnished desk affords should answer your needs.

On the other hand, if you're planning to decorate a tray, a chest or some other piece of furniture, you are going to need paints and varnishes, as well as scissors and paste, and the facilities for using them. Important even at the beginning is a space to work in, with a worktable and a file for a start (see Plate 71). As your projects grow more elaborate, so will your equipment. You will be amazed at your need for filing facilities and at their growing value to you.

Taking care of your prints and engravings, both in their cut and uncut states, is imperative. All your material should be filed and labeled, and a stamp book with glassine pages at hand to hold all your delicate cuttings. For the average print, a legal-size file is adequate. Large prints can be laid flat in an appropriate place. You will find that wide, shallow drawer space is essential. An architect's blueprint chest of drawers is perfect for this purpose. These can be bought used — and in quite good condition — for much less than when new. They provide good storage space for many other things you will need to keep flat. Special subsections can be built within each

144

71. Helen Hinchliffe's workroom

drawer. Old spool chests are also wonderful for storage, and are sometimes to be found in antique shops in the country (see Plate 71).

Drawer space is most important in your workshop. You should have a set of small drawers, preferably with glass or plastic fronts, so that you can lay hand quickly on whatever you wish to use. Every craftsman needs quantities of small items at hand. You will also need a cabinet or wall of built-in shelves to house your paints, varnishes, lacquers, solvents, and a variety of other can and bottle goods.

Your worktable should be comfortable and roomy and on the long side, so that you will have room for the quarter-inch plate glass you will need for a pasting surface, as well as other items you work with. There should be enough space for you to keep your brushes, paste, clean rags and tools well away from your pasting surface. A worktable of ideal height for this particular craft will reach your midriff as you sit on a normal chair. You will feel a little above the table as you sit, yet won't have to bend over as you work. This gives you better control in your cutting, pasting and designing; any other level of worktable is exhausting.

ORDER IN YOUR WORKROOM

Whatever else you do, keep your workroom orderly. Clean it up each time you use it. Brushes must never be left lying about with paste or paint on them. Put the paste brushes in a container of water (old marmalade jars are wonderful for this), if you expect to go on using them on a job. Wash them out thoroughly when you are finished for the day, and stand them on their wooden ends to dry. Brushes left resting on their bristles will curl and lose their points and cease to do their job properly. This applies to paintbrushes as well. Keep them in their proper solvent when using, and give them a bath in Carbona or Renuzit to clean them. A good craftsman has a wholesome regard for all the things he uses.

TOOLS AND SUPPLIES—HOW TO USE THEM

Here is your checklist of all the materials you will need for your work in decoupage:

| Cutters: | X-acto knives, 1 set | Cuticle scissors |
| | Straight scissors | Razor blades |

Adhesives: Water-soluble paste or glue

Duco cement

Adhesium glue size (a sizing, not a glue)

Papers: Construction paper, black, 2 sheets

white, 2 sheets

Packet of mixed colors, nine by twelve inches

Tracing paper, 1 pad or roll

Sandpaper, 3 sheets #00

3 sheets #1½ coarse

Emery cloth

Waxed carbon paper, white or yellow (at art stores)

Paints: Water colors

Japan colors, oil paints

Casein colors (for matte finish, picture frames)

Brushes: Round sable brushes, Nos. 1, 2, 5, 7

Pencils: #B for soft drawing

Charcoal sticks or pencils

Varnish: 1 quart of varnish, 1 quart of thinner (turpentine)

Lacquer: Brushing lacquer, 1 quart; solvent, 1 quart (to be bought as needed)

Spraying lacquer (extra-fast drying)

Miscellaneous necessaries:

Plate glass quarter-inch thick (size suitable for your worktable)

Protectoid, frosted, 1 sheet or roll

Small wallpaper roller

Tweezers, 2 pairs   Spray gun

Rottenstone (small amount)   One-foot rule

Rust remover (liquid)   Pair rubber gloves

Masking tape, one inch wide (used by architects)

Stik-tack discs

Small wooden tool of your own making, whittled flat at the end to look like a screwdriver, for smoothing after pasting (half-inch dowel cut two or three inches is ideal)

HOW TO USE YOUR TOOLS AND SUPPLIES

X-acto knives are sold in sets and used for deep corners and precision cutting.

Scissors and razors are used for cutting out, according to convenience.

Water-soluble paste or glue will be adequate for nearly all your pasting work.

Adhesium glue size is used on the underside of a cutout with printed matter on the back and prevents it from showing through when pasted.

Construction paper is used to fit over areas such as the front of drawers or tops of chests or tables, so that you may lay down your cutouts for placement as you work up your design. Other colored construction paper is used to cut basic shapes or forms such as a vase, bird cage or dresser, on which you build other decorative material. It comes in a full line of colors in sizes nine by twelve inches to twenty-four by thirty-six inches. The thin weight is suitable for masking areas around which you are working; the heavy one for basic cutouts or silhouettes.

Tracing paper comes in pads or rolls. You use it for setting up designs, for blocking in with charcoal in planning arrangements for large areas such as screen panels, murals or doors.

Sandpaper should be used to prepare the surface of a box, tray or piece of furniture so that it is smooth to the touch before painting. For a final rubdown on either a varnished or lacquered finish, use fine sandpaper before applying the last coat.

Waxed carbon paper, sold in art stores, is used for transferring a design to a tray or other hard surface.

*Paints: Water colors are used to paint shadows, to touch up edges and other parts of cutout prints which may have been damaged as you cut, sanded or pasted them. You may also need to draw or paint a connecting stem or other line that was too fine for cutting or for which you had no suitable material. Backgrounds may also need touching up.

Brushes will be useful for filling in with water color where necessary and usually for gluing; both jobs require a soft brush. A good brush always points well when wet and has plenty of spring when pushed back and forth with the finger.

Pencils, charcoal sticks are for blocking in designs.

* For further information on and applications for paint, varnish and lacquer, see end of this chapter.

*Varnish, with turpentine for solvent, will give your work a hard, lasting finish.

*Lacquer, and its solvent, is used for a quick-drying finish.

Miscellanies

Plate glass quarter-inch thick provides the surface on which you lay your work to paste it. It is easy to lift pasted pieces from the glass, and the glass itself is easy to clean.

Protectoid is used when taking off designs you may wish to have permanently in your files. (Always take some along when you go to a library.) One side is frosted, the other glossy and smooth. Trace on the frosted side. You can also make color notes on the frosted side using quick-drying japan colors.

Wallpaper roller will help you smooth out large areas of your work and press out air bubbles and excess glue. Your handmade dowel tool is to use on areas that need special pressure around the edges; a wooden instrument will not tear as you press.

Tweezers enable you to pick up cut pieces for easy placement in the design.

Stik-tack discs secure your work as you arrange it. They are particularly useful when you are working on standing pieces such as screens.

Masking tape will hold the edges of paper securely on large surfaces so that they will not curl when dry, then lifts off easily.

Emery cloth is used for rubbing down between coats of varnish or lacquer.

Rottenstone is used between coats of varnish. Try it this way: dip it in water, take it up in a soft rag, and rub circularwise over varnished surfaces that have been sanded. This smooths the varnish, building a wonderful surface.

Rust remover is an aid in cleaning up old rusty trays. It also prevents further rusting, and it is good for any new metal surfaces you may be painting. To be applied first.

Rubber gloves come in handy with many such procedures and in doing over old furniture. (See Chapter 12.)

Spray gun is to use for lacquer when you wish an extra fast drying surface.

Foot rule is necessary for accuracy in measuring arrangements before the final pasting, so that pairs of panels, for example, match exactly.

* For further information on and applications for varnish and lacquer, see end of this chapter.

PAINTS FOR BASE COATS

Before applying decoupage to trays, boxes and other accessories, whether of metal or wood, you will probably want to coat them with a fast drying flat paint. For this purpose, try japan paints, sold in tubes or small cans. The colors are limited but they do include those used by the old-time painters of trays, signs, chests and other household objects of early colonial America. These were once known as "coach colors" because coachmakers made liberal use of the red, blue, green and pumpkin yellow. When varnished, they took on a depth of tone that delighted the owners and travelers of the time. These coach colors make delectable pastels, or in-between shades, when lightened with a full-bodied flat white, such as the velour white of the makers of japan colors. Black in japan paint is, of course, an old stand-by.

The best coverage for large pieces such as a secretary, table, screen or built-in piece of furniture is a flat oil paint of standard make. Unless you've had some experience in mixing colors, have your local paint dealer do it for you. This will save hours of hard labor. All the dealer needs is a sample of the color you want on some matte surface such as paper, or a dull-finish fabric.

Casein and water colors mix well. They will do well used in any arrangement that will hang on the wall, to supplement the decoupage and for painting the frames, but not for furniture and other objects subject to wear and tear.

For painting eggs and any other small surfaces that must be done quickly — and for a good hard surface — use an art-supply store product called "Shower-Pruf Paint." It dries in ten minutes, is hard and firm in thirty minutes. (Turpentine will slow its drying.) For other base-coat paint mixtures see Chapter 12 on Pointers on Mixing Paints.

Remember that each coat of paint should dry for twenty-four hours before the next coat is applied. After the first coat, paint should be rubbed down with the finer grade of sandpaper. After the second coat, use a fine grade of emery cloth. Rottenstone will give you the best surface for the final finish, or an emery cloth, dampened.

FINISHING COATS

Methods of finishing decoupage vary with the project, as you have seen. The very flexibility of the medium allows for any number of different finishes. Some articles of furniture may require up to thirty coats of varnish or lacquer, while eight to ten coats may be enough for a tray. Pictures and murals may need no coat whatever. It's a matter of choice with a screen, although delicate components make one advisable. Framing with glass is protection enough for a picture or shadow box. And of course the glass itself is the protective surface of decoupage pasted on its underside.

You have seen in Chapter 5, on Pasting Up, that decoupage on furniture or on a tray, for example, calls for proper co-ordination between the base coat, the protective finishing coat, and the adhesive for pasting on your decoupage as well. Specifically, it is important how you combine these.

Say that you are decorating a wooden chest. If you have first covered it with oil paint for a base, you can with confidence apply a clear varnish for a final finishing coat: the solvent of the varnish will not affect the oil-paint base.

On the other hand, if you were to start with the oil-paint base and attempt to use lacquer for the final finish, you run the risk of ruining the whole thing because the solvent in lacquer can spoil a paint surface. This does not always happen; but lacquer on lacquer is safest, barring the ever-present hazard with lacquer finish that it may modify the colors on the face of your decoupage. (See Lacquer Finish in this chapter.)

As for the adhesive to use, one of the modern water-soluble pastes or glues recommended in the chapter on Paste Up is compatible with any one of these combinations.

VARNISH — FOR A LASTING SURFACE

For a durable, hard-wearing finish, you will probably find varnish superior to lacquer, especially if you are finishing decoupage on furniture, such as a table top or secretary, or on trays and other articles which see daily service. The varnishes on the market today are a vast improvement over those of prewar days. A great objection to the old varnish was that it gave everything a yellow cast. This was desirable, perhaps, in a period piece where a mellow antique effect was sought. But for the most part, people prefer a clear, fresh color. The new varnishes make this possible; they now are almost as clear as lacquer, even though they look yellow when first applied. The yellow cast disappears in the drying, which takes at least four hours on a clear, dry day. This, by the way, is the only kind of weather in which to apply either varnish or lacquer.

There are some who think varnish after four hours is dry enough to take another coat. In working with decoupage, however, the safe and sound way is to wait a full twenty-four hours, so that the solvent can evaporate completely. Take your time with finishes: this is a cardinal principle.

Varnish, like paint, should be rubbed down after each coat. Use fine sandpaper, emery cloth, or a fine abrasive like rottenstone on the final coat.

Both high-gloss and dull-finish varnishes are available. Each has its use, and four to ten coats of either one should give your work all the protection it needs. Variation in the thickness of papers used in decoupage had a lot to do with the number of coats of varnish advocated in the past. Some still insist on thirty to fifty misted coats. But if you select your materials so that the edges are of a matched thickness, so that your project has an allover consistency in depth, it will not require such extensive surfacing. There is always, however, room for divergence of opinion and personal preference in this matter.

You hear a good deal about table- and bar-top finishes that are alcohol-proof. Actually, the watered alcohol that spills on a varnished table is negligible and so weak it couldn't make the slightest impression on the surface. Only strong solutions of alcohol and other solvents affect a varnished finish, and that only if left on for a time. The new types of varnish are impervious to water. Incidentally, white rings, cup imprints, hot-dish marks and scratches on old varnished tops can be removed by using Scratch Fixing Liquid, procurable in paint and hardware stores. There are several such products.

LACQUER FINISH

A lacquer finish, which is not considered as durable as varnish, is appropriate for surfaces that will receive little handling. It gives a clear, bright, hard finish which will not, however, stand up to the daily beating a varnished surface will take. A lacquer finish can be completely satisfactory, subject to atmospheric conditions: overheated rooms as well as sudden changes in the weather can cause it to crack and peel. It can't take cigarette burns or other extreme heat; when damaged, it is hard to repair. Lacquer is popular with commercial users and others because its solvent evaporates quickly, permitting it to dry in a few minutes in dry weather. Several thin coats can be brushed or sprayed on over a short period of time, thus speeding up the work. This is an advantage when you realize that up to thirty or more coats may be required on certain pieces of furniture. It is wise, nevertheless, to let lacquer dry for at least an hour between applications.

If you are planning a final lacquered finish for your decoupage project, you would be well advised to start with a lacquer base for it. You can either brush this on or spray it on, in whatever color you choose. Lacquers are available in colors as well as clear. Give the base at least three coats; more are desirable. It is not necessary to rub down lacquer; it dries practically on contact and scarcely has time to gather dust particles.

When the base coats have dried thoroughly, apply your cutouts, preferably with one of the modern water-soluble pastes. After the drying period, brush on the clear lacquer. Brushing lacquers contain a slow-drying solvent which gives you time to "flow" on the color or the clear finish. A little practice will teach you how much to take up on your brush. Always "flow" or brush the lacquer in one direction.

Lacquer, as noted above, can also be sprayed on. This requires a spray gun, an open window so the fumes of the lacquer's highly volatile solvent can escape, and a table on which you can put a carton large enough to contain the object you are spraying. It will be easier to get even coverage if you can set in the carton a small "turntable" such as a Lazy Susan, so that you can spin your work as you spray it. All sprays should be misted on — that is, a quick once-over. Don't let the spray linger, as it were.

The technique of misting on a very fine coat of lacquer is one that you should master and is the only way you can hope to succeed when lacquering over a paint base, always a tricky procedure. (See above on Finishing Coats.) This can be and has been done with skilled use of the spray gun. The first two or three coats should be as fine and thin as is mechanically possible. After these have, so to speak, "sealed off" the base coat, you can continue to spray on additional coats with some sense of security. You may even return to the brushing method if you prefer. It is only through practice and infinite restraint in these matters that you will be able to turn out lasting — and flawless — work.

Spraying lacquers now available in paint and hardware stores are good if the colors are right for your project. You can get interesting effects of your own by combining colors, such as deep green, sprayed with light yellow, then white.

DUSTPROOF ROUTINE

During the drying periods, both of base-paint coats and finishing coats of varnish or lacquer, every project must be protected as far as possible from dust particles. Not everyone can afford the luxury of dust-free rooms. However you can take steps to approximate it.

Clean your workroom by vacuum, never by old-fashioned sweeping and dusting. Work with lint-free rags only. Avoid wearing woolen garments that can shed particles of fiber; a good cotton coverall should help solve your problem. When spraying lacquer, especially, you will find there is hardly time to remove such minute foreign bodies before it is too late.

Another most important precaution is to put projects under a table large enough to cover them. There should be plenty of room all around them so that when you throw a sheet over the table it does not come in contact with the work. The cloth gives a fair amount of protection from dust. Your paint or varnish dries well even though shielded from free circulation of air.

CHAPTER 12

Methods and Formulas

DECOUPAGE ON GLASS

Glass can be decorated with decoupage either on the top surface or on the underside. The difference in pasting on the underside of glass is that your water-soluble paste should be diluted, not used full strength. This is so that it may be as invisible as possible, since the paste is spread on the face of the cutouts instead of on the back. First put the paste in a saucer and add a few drops of boiling water, until you have the desired consistency. This will call for a little experimentation on your part, on a separate piece of glass.

Decoupage on the underside of glass provides your work with permanent protection and obviates the necessity for applying the many coats of varnish or lacquer required for otherwise unprotected surfaces. Decoupage on the underside of glass is well suited for table tops, dressing tables, screens, wastebaskets, boxes, mirror frames and lamp bases.

SELECTING THE GLASS

There are three thicknesses of glass suitable for decoupage decoration. For some projects the lightweight, one-sixteenth-inch thickness is best but too thin for others. The windowpane thickness, an eighth of an inch, is good for box tops, pictures and lightweight screens. The quarter-inch thickness, known as plate glass, can be used for dining tables and other substantial projects. Plate glass can be cut flush or given a beveled edge, depending on how you wish to use it. If it is for a coffee table or similar use, it can be beveled, but remember that beveling a glass edge tends to weaken it and may lead to small chips and bruises known as "blushes." It is fairly safe to have the edges of wall sconces beveled.

CLEANING THE GLASS

Your greatest concern, actually, in working with glass is to have a one hundred per cent clean surface on which to paste your decoupage arrangement. Nothing is so maddening as the discovery, after you have pasted up, of a dirty smear or thumbmark right on the middle of a cutout. It can't be cleaned, of course, unless you strip the whole thing and start over again.

Working on a table — the full length of the glass if possible — you first cover it with plenty of newspapers. Lay the glass on the table and sprinkle cleanser or pulverized pumice all over it. Dip a sponge into warm soapy water, to which you have added a teaspoonful of ammonia, and begin washing it. Any stubborn oil or other foreign matter can be removed with a bit of steel wool. Now turn the glass over and repeat the process on the other side. When the glass feels smooth to your finger tips on both sides and free from all dirt, pick it up and set it in a tub for the final rinsing.

THE FINAL RINSING

If you are working with a large piece of glass, put a rubber mat on the floor of the tub and stand the glass on it, at a slant, against the wall. Small pieces of glass can be cleaned in a basin or sink and should also be placed on a rubber mat to prevent chipping or cracking at the corners.

Rinsing water should be poured over the glass and should be hot but not boiling. When the glass is free of all soap and cleanser, leave it to drain. Now change the newspapers on your worktable, replacing them with fresh. Give the glass a good polish on both sides. Pick it up using a heavy bath towel so as to avoid finger marks where you hold it, and lay it once more on the table.

THE USE OF GUIDELINES

Guidelines are a great help in working up a design of any size on glass. They will serve to direct you in measuring distance and charting accurate placement of the cutout elements when you start transferring your design from the tracing paper (see Chapter 4 on How to Set Up a Design).

With a colored grease crayon draw a line vertically dead center the full length of the glass, another horizontally dead center the full width of the glass. Remember that this is on the surface not to be pasted. The lines drawn on the glass are to correspond exactly with the lines you have drawn on the tracing paper on which you are setting up the preliminary layout for your design. For additional guidance, you may draw two more lines, centered at each side of the vertical line. This gives you three lines running up and down. Repeat your horizontal lines in the same way and you will have three lines running across the glass. You may add as many more lines as you need running up and down and across, drawing them, of course, so they correspond exactly with the lines on the tracing paper.

When you have finished marking the guidelines, put, under each corner of the glass, a block or books of equal height to hold it up evenly and free it all around at least six inches from the table top. It is now ready for you to paste your decoupage arrangement on the underside, with enough room for your hands to operate from below.

PASTING ON GLASS

Assuming that you have already set up your design on tracing paper, you will find it a simple matter to make the transfer. In the case of a floral arrangement, or any other subject that entails the use of a number of separate pieces, your first selection for pasting should be one that will have nothing superimposed on its surface, as a leaf or a tendril might. In your pasting, that is, work from the immediate foreground toward the background. Large single units like the figure used in the screen (Plate 47) present no such problem. Their position and their alignment are simply measured and checked.

In pasting on glass (see Chapter 5) you should spread the paste evenly but thinly, dipping your brush in water first, then into the paste. And no matter what the size of the cutout, make very sure that each piece is free of bubbles as you press it on gently, using a damp cloth, and working always from the center to the edges. When you have completed the pasting on of your design, let it dry for twenty-four hours. Then do your cleanup job. If you plan to use paint for a background, first give the back of the decoupage arrangement a coat of white paint, taking pains to let no paint spread beyond the edges. When this has dried, apply a coat of varnish over the entire underside surface. Then, after the usual drying period, apply a coat of paint of whatever color you've chosen.

CHOICE OF BACKGROUNDS

There are several ways to supply a background for your work:

(1) You can give it a silver or gold-leaf ground (see Gilding, this chapter).

(2) You can paint in a background in any flat oil paint. If you paint it, make doubly sure first that every edge is firmly stuck to the glass so that no paint can seep through onto your decoupage, and follow instructions above.

(3) You can cover the surface the glass will rest on with fabric or decorative paper.

When you use fabric or paper as a background for your decoupage under glass, it is usually for a recessed or paneled setting, such as the panel of a screen, in which the glass is to be placed. Cut the material to fit as nearly possible by putting it under the glass and cutting the outline with an Exacto knife. If you're not handy with the knife, draw a pencil line around the edge and cut it out with scissors. Then put the material in position in its panel and secure the top corners with thumbtacks, making sure that it hangs straight. Using a small amount of paste, start brushing it on across the top of the panel. Then apply the material and, using a dry cloth, hold it in place until the paste has set firmly. Be sure to pick up paste sparingly on your brush, otherwise it will show through the fabric or paper when it has dried.

Continue thus on down the panel, pasting until finished, and let it dry overnight. Give the glass a thorough going over, examining it from all angles against the light to be sure no smears or marks remain. Then set it in its place.

The glass can be secured with a narrow half-round molding, with mitered corners, painted the same color as the rest of the screen, and can be nailed at frequent intervals to the frame. It's a good idea to have a woodworker do this for you. If you're not an expert, you run the risk of cracking the glass. Another method is to have your glazier drill holes in the four corners of the glass which then can be secured to the frame with glass screws obtainable at hardware stores.

Many persons hesitate to work with glass lest it cut them, or break, or be too heavy to handle or too hard to frame. Some of these objections hold a grain of truth, but most of them are imaginary. Glass like any other substance has its idiosyncrasies. The trick is to control glass with your mind, not altogether with your hands.

In handling glass be gentle with it, relaxed. Never press the hands to its edges, holding it like grim death. If you do, you certainly will get cut. If the sides of a piece of glass are too rough to handle while you are washing it, wear rubber or heavy cotton gloves. When your glazier cuts a new piece of glass for you, have him smooth the edges; it's a big help. After a little practice your difficulties with glass, real or imagined, will melt away.

POTICHOMANIA

As noted in Chapter 1, potichomania is a word — French in origin — for the fad of pasting colored cutouts on glass vessels, which flourished during the first half of the nineteenth-century. (*Potiche* is French for Oriental vase, *manie* is mania.) This craze originated in France but hit its peak of popularity in England. Like *l'arte del povero*, the Italian phrase for decoupage, potichomania was for those who could not afford expensive Sèvres china or the even more costly Chinese porcelains, and was done on glass to imitate these.

Glass vases or globes with openings at one end or both large enough to admit the hand were decorated on the inside with paper cutouts. When the paste-up was dry, the cutouts were backed with a coat of paint, the vessel filled with sand and used as an ornament for the mantelpiece. Sometimes the vase was decorated by pasting colored cutouts on the outside, given a coat of varnish for protection and used to hold flowers. In England these were known as Dolly Varden jars. Later, when this kind of handicraft degenerated into pasting cigar bands on the underside of glass ash trays, it died out.

DECOUPAGE

Today a version of potichomania is reappearing in lamp bases and candle holders, with the cutouts pasted on the inside. Glass lamp bases usually have a good-sized opening at both ends so that you can use both hands and paste up your decoupage with relative ease. Using the diluted consistency of the water-soluble paste, you spread it thinly on the face of your cutouts and press them onto the glass. (See Chapter 5 on Pasting Up.) When the paste-up is dry, clean the glass thoroughly and give the back of the decoupage work a protecting coat of paint. Don't let the paint smear over the edges onto the glass; or if it does, clean it off using turpentine with a bit of cotton on a toothpick. After drying period, clean the entire inside of the lamp base and apply a coat of varnish over all. When this is dry, select your background color, using a quick-drying paint like tempera or japan paint; both adhere well. Then take your lamp to a lampman for mounting and you will have a useful and decorative accessory which expresses your own taste and individuality.

For goblets to hold candles you may follow the same procedure. Or if you prefer, skip the paint backing and leave the glass clear. But do give a coat of paint to the back of the decoupage work itself for that necessary protection.

You may wish to carry your experimenting further for a waterproof glass container. In that case, you should proceed as with the lamp base, choosing an over-all paint background. When your decoupage work has been protected with the layers of paint and varnish, according to the procedure outlined above, you may add as many coats of varnish as you choose. You may then use your container for holding flowers or small plants, resting assured that you have built up a surface that will hold water.

RENOVATING SURFACES FOR DECOUPAGE

Preparing an old piece of furniture, a wooden box, a metal tray, or any used paint-covered article you have chosen to decorate with paper cutouts starts with paint remover. Even a piece that has not been painted but waxed over the years must have the wax removed. Paint remover will accomplish this and is less work and more foolproof than the usual method of washing down an old surface with turpentine or other solvent.

Metal hardware on a box or piece of furniture should be removed before you start stripping it. Put all the hardware, including the screws, into a container and set it safely aside. Sometimes you will find the hardware on old pieces is irreplaceable.

The only way to do anything in life with a reasonable degree of success and comfort is to be properly booted and spurred. In doing over an old piece you will need rubber gloves, steel wool #1, lots of old newspapers, lots of rags, and Renuzit: these are your boots and spurs. You will find a complete list at the end of this section.

The cream type of remover, in any well-known brand, is best to use, since it does not run after it is brushed on. Use your coarse 1½-inch brush for the purpose and throw it away afterward; these brushes are inexpensive and not worth cleaning. Work somewhere near the open air, as paint remover is volatile, and fumes need to escape. If you can work in the garage or some other spot where you needn't worry about the floor, fine—you won't have to be so fussy. But if you have to do this job in rather close quarters, take a corner near a window, and put lots of newspapers under and well around the project. You might even put down an old shower curtain first. (Save them for just such uses.) Paint remover eats through almost anything that may happen to be lying around, and the curtain is one more protection.

Leave the remover on for an hour and then with your #1 steel wool and a spatula start lifting the old finish. It really goes quite quickly and is not the chore people think it. For pieces that have turned legs or are carved, wrap the steel wool around the turning and then rub gently. For carving of this sort a small wire brush does the job in no time. Do not dig into the wood, for that might leave scratches. Use it with a light "picking-it-up" touch and all will be well.

When all surfaces are free from paint, pour Renuzit or turpentine into a can, dip in your steel wool and clean the entire piece of all residue. Don't worry about old stains that may remain in the wood fibers. They will not show when painted.

When the piece is all smooth and ready for paint, go over it to see if there are any old nail holes or cracks or broken pieces that need filling or mending. Nail holes and cracks may be filled with wood filler, while broken pieces must be replaced. Let the wood filler dry thoroughly and then sand it, against the grain, until its surface is as smooth as the rest of the piece.

SURFACING NEW PIECES

An unpainted piece of furniture must have a coat of shellac first, then be allowed to dry twenty-four hours. Next, sand it lightly, and when the surface has been dusted off, give it another coat of shellac. Orange shellac is quite good enough for this purpose. Let this coat dry twenty-four hours and sand again until quite smooth. Unless it, too, needs wood filler here and there, it is ready for painting.

Paint today is not the color problem it used to be; many firms present a full line of what they call "decorator colors." Take a sample of the special color you have in mind to your paint dealer, and chances are he will have it for you. Enamels also are available in a much better color range than formerly. If your paint store hasn't it, try an auto-supply firm; they usually carry a full line. In the old days you had to start with quite light colors to allow for the darkening effect of a coat or two of varnish. (You should remember this change if you are doing a piece of work that must look antique.) But the average job will turn out to be the color you wanted, for the clear varnishes of today don't affect the tone.

Two coats, three at most, are adequate for any paint job you might tackle. When using lacquer, spray it on large pieces, but brush it on smaller ones. Your soft 2½-inch brush is the one to use for oil paint as well as lacquer. Be good to the brush; see that it remains in its solvent when not in use and that it is cleaned at the end of the day. A brush lasts longer if cared for, and these particular brushes are not cheap.

POINTERS ON MIXING PAINTS

It is quite possible that you may someday wish to give a project a base coat of paint in an unusual color, as an accent in its room setting, or to pick up a tone from a rug, a painting or the curtains. For those experienced in—or wanting to learn about—mixing oil paint, the following combinations may prove of interest. Start with these basics and, if they please you, it is a simple matter to experiment with others from time to time:

Chrome yellow light, chrome yellow medium, Prussian blue, red, burnt sienna, raw umber, chrome green dark, lampblack or ivory black, velour white (nothing less than quart size of velour white is sold).

162

Mix with #2 brush, using turpentine for your thinner. Use rags to keep the brush clean; also for cleaning it between painting sessions.

No. 1 Mix: Mix small amounts of chrome green and Prussian blue, with the least bit of raw umber added. Lighten with velour white until desired shade is arrived at—makes a wonderful off-shade blue.

No. 2 Mix: Chrome yellow light and Prussian blue give you a brilliant leaf green. If you wish to tone it down, proceed as above with white and umber.

No. 3 Mix: Burnt sienna (a small amount) and velour white produce a good pink. Nothing else need be added.

No. 4 Mix: Red and chrome yellow and a small amount of umber add up to an exciting off-shade pumpkin color. Use very little red. Lighten with white and see what you get.

BLEACHING WOOD

If instead of painting a wood surface you wish to bleach it, proceed as follows: For small pieces which can be put into a bucket, fill the bucket with water and add two parts fox paste to one part lye. Let the wood pieces remain there overnight. If then they are not bleached as much as you wish, leave them for several hours longer or until they suit you. Then wash them in cold water and dry them in the sun if possible; this will bleach them further.

Large pieces can be bleached by brushing them with the same solution, keeping them wet by frequent applications. The bleaching process described here will remove old paint at the same time.

MATERIALS AND TOOLS FOR REMOVING PAINT

Pair of rubber gloves	Painter's spatula	Small wire brush
Roll of #1 steel wool	Cream or liquid paint remover	Turpentine
Orange shellac	Paint	Renuzit

Brushes: one-inch fitch or oxtail for small pieces; 1½- to 2-inch soft oxtail or fitch for painting; 1½-inch coarse for applying paint remover. Old shower curtain (optional)

Sandpaper sheets, 3 fine, 3 medium coarse
Wooden tongue spatulas, for mixing paint in small quantities
Empty cans
Old newspapers and rags

GILDING

Gilding is for the lily in decoupage. It is also for the experts and is a highly paid, skilled trade. People working with gold leaf do so in rooms completely free from dust and drafts. Since gold leaf must be picked up with a special brush and deftly laid upon a velvet cushion—from which it is then transferred to the object being decorated—the slightest draft defeats the entire operation.

However, it is effective in decoupage, and there is a metal leaf for the amateur, an alloy called "Dutch metal." Made in Germany and Italy, it is relatively inexpensive and can be worked fairly easily with excellent results.

Dutch metal is sold in square books, ranging in size from two to five inches, each leaf between sheets of tissue. It comes in several shades of gold, from bright lemon-yellow to a deep Roman gold. You can get a sheet in variegated tones of fire red and deep purple blended with brilliant green. It is most effective for decorating boxes, screen borders, mirrors or Christmas cards. The glittering colors can be toned down in an interesting fashion with a coat of lacquer or varnish. (If for any project you need a silver shade, use aluminum foil.)

As an adhesive for the metal leaf, you use gold size, obtainable at art stores. This is spread on the surface where you intend to apply the gold and allowed to dry (overnight) until it reaches that tacky point when it clicks at a touch of the finger but still is sticky enough to hold the gold leaf (see Sources of Supply).

Dutch metal can be applied directly from the sheet of tissue paper it rests on. Cut your book on the folded side so that each leaf can be picked up easily. Be sure that your fingers are clean when you handle it, because it will stick to anything. A gentle breath will blow out any turned corners and flatten them again.

Handling leaf for the first time, you will feel awkward and apprehensive. When it's imperfectly laid and perhaps cracks in the process, you will think you have botched everything. But even the experts have to patch up a crack with another piece laid on top. Besides, cracks, a few wrinkles and tears here and there can give an interesting look of age. Don't quarrel with such an effect, provided it is controlled and not sloppy.

Like any new effort, laying metal leaf has to have a tryout. For a rough beginning, try lifting the tissue and leaf with leaf facing the object you are decorating.

Hold it with the thumb and forefinger of the right hand at the top corner, with the left hand at the bottom corner. Lift it directly over your project, place it exactly where you want it, then remove the tissue. It is best at first to work with small two- by two-inch pieces, for you can control this size more easily than the larger sizes which can come later. You can, of course, cut the metal leaf into any smaller sizes and shapes you need.

When you have finished a session of laying in the gold leaf, put your work aside for at least twenty-four hours. It should be completely dry before you do anything further on it. Use a soft brush to pick up the loose gold and brush it into a screw-top jar. The leavings will come in handy for patching and other small jobs in the future.

TO SPEED UP GOLD-LEAFING

If you wish to apply gold leaf in small areas on a wood or metal surface, and do not wish to hold up the rest of the project unduly, prepare a small amount of the following formula: one ounce of fast-drying gold size combined with one-quarter ounce of slow-drying varnish. Brush this on the areas you wish to gild, and when the solution has dried to the tacky stage, apply the gold leaf.

GOLD-LEAFING ON GLASS

If you wish to apply gold leaf to glass, the formula for sizing the surface is as follows: Pour cold water, one inch deep, into a cup. Sprinkle enough clear gelatin on it to cover the surface. Let it stand ten minutes, or until dissolved, and add hot water almost to fill the cup. Let it cool, then stir it and brush it on the area the size of each leaf you use. Continue this procedure until the project is completed.

MARBLING PAPER

Marbling paper is one of the most desirable and useful of decorative papers for decoupage. You can buy it (see Sources of Supply) or you can make it yourself by one of several simple methods. Select a good rag paper for the purpose. Make your choice of oil color, or colors, and thin with Renuzit or any good cleaning fluid. Float the fluid on a pan of water large enough to take the full sheet of paper.

Now with a feather tip draw swirls or other forms of design in the solution. Lay your paper on and draw it across the pan, then place it face up on a flat surface to dry. When it is dry, you may iron it between sheets of paper, if you wish, or use it as it is. It makes little difference, since applying it to a pasted surface will smooth it out.

Some amateurs have found it helpful to use for the solution cold water that rice has been boiled in; the slight viscosity of this fluid tends to control the swirls of paint and "holds" the pattern in place while you are laying on the paper. Professionals sometimes use a gelatinlike solution of carageen moss, a seaweed that grows off the coast of Ireland. This is bleached in the sun, then boiled in water to produce a viscous solution or size. On this they float specially prepared water colors and use a comb or stick to draw the pattern.

EGG-YOLK "LACQUER"

For an especially rich, hard-finishing coat for boxes or other surfaces try the following formula: Separate the yolk of an egg from the white. Into a jar with a screw top, strain the egg yolk, piercing its outer membrane with a fork. (Be sure this skin does not fall into the jar.) Add about two tablespoons of cold water and shake well until blended.

To give the mixture the right color, add a tiny bit of water-soluble raw umber or burnt umber. Raw umber provides the real antique coloring, but burnt umber gives it a soft, pinkish tone, sometimes very desirable. It is a good idea to experiment for tone value.

Apply this mixture to the object you are finishing with one-way brush strokes. Don't try to use it as you would paint; it would pile up and be messy. Use a wide, soft brush so that it is spread on quickly, with complete coverage, and let it dry for twenty-four hours. This finish can be applied to gold paper trim and other paper surfaces also.

JAPANNED SURFACE

For a base coat on boxes or other objects for which you plan decoupage, you can use the following formula: To one-half cup of gold size, add enough lampblack oil paint to give it intensity. The gold size can be either the fast-drying or the slow-drying type. Let either one dry for twenty-four hours and you will have a good glossy surface to paste your decoupage on. It will require no other coat of varnish or lacquer.

SKELETONIZING LEAVES

Skeletonized leaves are good for filling in backgrounds of flower or shell decoupage arrangements. They are effective also for composing delicate diaphanous patterns between sheets of plastic for screens or place mats.

There are two ways to bleach and skeletonize them:

(1) If you have a yard or some outside area, put your selection of leaves in a wooden bucket, cover them with water and weight them down under a piece of glass. Leave them undisturbed for from four to six weeks, adding water as needed so that it does not sink below the level of the leaves during this period.

When the leaves look the way you want them to, lay them out, leaf by leaf, in the sun to dry. Then press them carefully with a warm iron between sheets of brown paper. They are ready now to be stored between sheets of paper for future use.

(2) You can bleach and skeletonize leaves by soaking them in a solution made by dissolving four ounces of chloride of lime, or chloride of soda, in a pint of water. For very delicate leaves, make a slightly weaker solution by adding about a half-pint more water.

Put the leaves in this solution in a glass container and leave them there for a few hours or until they are bleached to suit you. Next, wash them thoroughly in fresh cold water and lay them aside for drying. Then press them flat and store them, as described above.

Leaves in the following classifications will provide interesting and decorative shapes; experience will teach you how to bleach them to the desired degree: *Vines:* ivy, bignonia, wistaria. *Trees and shrubs:* maple, magnolia, ash, beech, chestnut, elm, pomegranate, witch hazel, rose, lemon. *Evergreens:* holly, barberry, rhododendron, camellia japonica. The last-named leaf can be treated by boiling in a solution of soap and water. Peel off the skin and dry in the sun as noted above.

DECOUPAGE

FERNS, MOSSES, LICHENS

Collecting small ferns, mosses, lichens and other minute plants from the forest, the rocky coasts and other quiet places where they grow requires a selective eye. The process of preparing them for decoupage, however, is a relatively simple one. Making a collection can of itself be an interesting pursuit, made infinitely more so by a study of their classifications. This, incidentally, would prove helpful when you come to sorting and putting the plants away for future use. In a book which tells you about this wonderful world, *The Story of Mosses, Ferns and Mushrooms,* Dorothy Sterling offers you the spellbinding information that millions of years ago these tiny miniatures of plant life actually were the denizens of giant green forests.

Ferns, mosses, skeletonized leaves, small flowers, stems and tendrils supply many of the necessary components of flower pictures, shell pictures and other decoupage decoration. They can be used for charming free arrangements between laminated plastic sheets for screens and place mats, or under glass for box tops or coffee tables. Along the rocky coast of Maine where she spends her summers, Mrs. Mary Brown Moon collects her woodland material. She sorts her harvest very carefully and classifies each piece. Then they are laid flat, face down, on sheets of thin cardboard or blotting paper which are piled carefully on top of each other. Finally they are clamped down in a large book press and left to flatten and dry for several weeks. Since drying time varies, she examines them after a few weeks to see if they are ready. When they look right, she places them gently between sheets of tissue paper and puts them in boxes to be labeled according to the classification of the plants they contain.

PREPARING GARDEN FLOWERS

Living flowers picked from your own garden can be processed in your kitchen oven to retain their color and to provide yet another material for decorative arrangement and paste-up. Baking flowers together with some leaves or ferns in sterilized white sand at low temperatures in your oven is not difficult, but it may take some experiments to find out which flowers you succeed best with, as well as which take less cooking than others.

In the first place, single flowers and the flatter shapes are easiest to work with: pansies, daisies, cosmos, larkspur, Queen Anne's lace, baby's breath, asters, forget-me-nots and any others you may like to try. Pick flowers at their peak and only those that are unblemished. Pick them dry, not when they're damp with dew or after rain. When you have collected your quota for the day, start processing them at once.

One thing to remember when you are collecting a batch is to cut buds of each kind and have extra stems. Pick these with the long-stemmed flowers. You will need many such aids, when you come to arrange your bouquet for pasting, to keep it graceful, airy and alive. If you have no dried ferns or skeletonized leaves, buy some asparagus fern from the florist. Bake these in the pan with the stems, at the same time experimenting with other ferns and leaves.

Select two pans, about three inches deep—any that you may happen to have, tin or enamel or Pyrex. Use one for flowers, one for ferns and stems. Into each one pour sand to the depth of one inch. (Sterilized sand is sold with children's sand-boxes, or buy it from your builder; ordinary beach sand won't do.) Lay each flower on the sand—face down—and with your hand gently dust over the lot with sand. You should shove a little extra sand under each flower so that it won't dry too flat. Then cover both pans with another inch of sand, very carefully.

Next put your pans into the oven which should be kept at an even temperature of 200 degrees Fahrenheit. Most flowers take two hours of baking, but white flowers may turn yellow if left that long. Start testing them about an hour and a half after you've put them in.

To test the flowers, pour off a little sand at one end of the pan and with tweezers, very, very gently remove one. For easy handling you will find it wise to have left about one inch of stem on each which can be cut off before pasting. If the flower looks dark and dull, you have baked your batch too long. If, on the other hand, it is damp and limp, the flowers have not had enough time in the oven and must go back for more.

When the flowers look as they did after picking, they are just right. Take the pans out of the oven and let them cool off completely. At this stage they are at their most fragile and should not be touched until the sand has cooled to room temperature. Then you may carefully remove the upper sand and the flowers, gently brushing off any remaining sand particles with a soft paintbrush. At this point they are ready to be classified and stored as were the woodland material, although some prefer to make the flower picture at once.

A flower arrangement can be mounted on heavy paper, white or pastel, before framing, but it will be more elegant set against a delicate fabric background —velvet, satin, or organdy over satin, well stretched on a frame, in a shade that will harmonize with the interior where it will hang. A beading of small pearls around the inside of the frame, or a gold-embossed paper border will enhance the arrangement. When it is framed under glass, remember that the flowers should not touch the glass. Convex glass is attractive for a frame with a little depth but not necessary for a deeply set one. The same treatment holds for a coffee table or a shadow-box top.

In arranging your composition, try out the material you are going to use in various positions, finding where the flowers look best. Remember to use restraint, never overcrowd a piece. When you are satisfied with the arrangement, start with the underlying stems and fern and with a small amount of glue paste them into position.

Also, do not paste on any of the flowers with more than a little dab of glue at the center. All edges must be kept free for stems or other foliage that will be set back of the petals or at their points. Never let stems hang in a set and unnatural pattern at the bottom of your bouquet—held in the hand, a bouquet will show the stems crossing and overlapping each other; and not too many of these, either, perhaps five or six.

Around the edges of your bouquet, keep the outline feathery and lacy in feeling. Leave room for additional buds and leaves until you are sure the composition is complete. Even when it is finished, there should be as many edges as possible free of pasting. It gives the arrangement a lifelike air, and makes for the three-dimensional look so desirable in any decoupage rendering under glass. Be sure that the finished work is framed to be dust- and airtight. Flower pictures should have proper sealed construction to protect them from dirt and discoloration. This is best done by pasting heavy brown paper on the back of the frame and sealing the edges with paper tape.

QUILLWORK

Quillwork was one of the minor decorative arts, practiced in Europe from the seventeenth to the mid-eighteenth century, which found exponents in this country as well. Plate 72 shows one of a pair of sconces with intricate quillwork. These were made by Eunice Deering of Kittery, Maine, around 1730, and are now in the American Wing of the Metropolitan Museum of Art.

Quillwork, or filigree as it has been called, was done by rolling narrow strips of paper into spirals, volutes, scrolls or cone shapes which were sometimes colored or gilded and pasted into compositions of various sorts as added decoration, particularly for borders. This work looked so much like metal that it has been called "gold filigree" even by some of the experts. Much of the early work was made of strips of creamy vellum which, in its more intricate forms, has been mistaken for the old carved ivory pieces of the Middle Ages, or the pierced and lacquered boxes from ancient Persia. It was much used in multicolor, with the effect of mosaic, first for Teutonic heraldic devices, later in Italy, Spain and France for various decorative uses.

In the sconce shown in Plate 72 quillwork has been used in complicated figures for a border around the inside of the frame. It forms the three circular "flowers" at the top of the candle, and above it, right and left, the conelike formations also floral in aspect. In this instance, the paper has been gilded or gold-leafed and highly burnished. Some of the cones stand out in relief over an inch high, looking fantastically like real gold spikes. In the running design that forms the border, the paper has been used in single strands connecting the scroll-like bundles and florets, rather resembling uncoiled watch springs. The rest of the picture is composed of mica, shells, wax and other colorful substances including copper and silver wire, all assembled within a gilt wooden frame. With candles lighted, these sconces become glowing ornaments at once lavish and interesting.

This work became a social pastime in England right up to the days of Jane Austen, and beyond. It was eminently suited to amateurs. It lent great color and richness in its many various applications, as well as the look of antiquity. And it was relatively easy to do.

72. Early American sconce with borders and scrolls of quillwork

The paper in much of the early work had to be laboriously prepared. Usually it was painted and/or the edges gold-leafed. Nowadays you can provide yourself with paper strips already gold-leafed from old volumes which may have become otherwise expendable. One such book, if it's a thick one, should afford a wealth of material for several projects.

If you wish to try your hand at quillwork, decide on the object you wish to decorate or to supplement with quillwork, remembering that it is ideal for borders and fill-ins, and much better under glass than not. You might decide on a box top with a central motif in quillwork—combined with shells, perhaps—and corners to balance.

Make a rough sketch of your projected design so that you will have a fair idea of the amount of material you will need. Then cut the gold-leafed edge the full length of a page into a strip about an eighth of an inch wide. Start rolling the strip very tightly on the tip end of a toothpick. Don't make these rolls too thick. You might get as much as two forms out of each strip; this you will discover for yourself as you work. Remove the toothpick carefully and draw out the paper roll into the shape you wish. Touch the underside of it with glue and place it at the center, or as a petal or whatever, in the design you have planned. Continue from there on until you have filled in as desired. Small shells, pearls, stones, bits of mother-of-pearl or whatever you choose can be used to complete or extend the composition.

EGGSHELLS FOR DECOUPAGE

The delicate surface of the eggshell is a tempting one for decoupage, but its very fragility has been a deterrent to many. And indeed eggshells aren't what they're cracked up to be anymore, what with the enterprising poultryman and stepped-up production in the henhouse: the poor hens haven't time to ingest or store up enough calcium or lime, or whatever it is they make their eggshells with. As everyone knows, eggshells today shatter at the slightest tap. However, with care and luck, you may set a fair average of success with them.

To decorate a whole egg, you must first empty it. This is done by making holes at each end of the egg large enough so that it will drain, perhaps using a darning needle. When the egg seems to be empty, blow it out through one end so as to be sure, then rinse it with warm water. Let it dry thoroughly before you start work on it. You will, of course, later find it necessary to paste decoration of some sort over the holes you have made.

Duck and hen eggs are naturally easiest to buy, but it's worth the effort to hunt for ostrich eggs and the eggs of wild game birds. It would be a mistake to paint the outside surfaces of these, since they have exquisite colorings of their own, and often interesting spotted designs as well. The inside of the egg may be delicately colored and the edges decorated with gold trim and tiny floral or gold motifs scattered inside for added interest and glitter.

To cut an egg in half, draw a fine pencil line around its middle circumference and tape the edge of your pencil line on each side. Place the egg over a saucer to catch the contents neatly and start cutting with care. For cutting, if you can get a jeweler's saw, so much the better; if not, ask your chemist for the blade that cuts the neck of the ampule.

Another method that works more than reasonably well is to brush on a band of paraffin, about an inch wide, around the middle of the egg. Mark a line around the egg in the center of the paraffin band. Then with a needle, prick all along this line a continuous succession of tiny holes until you can gently pry the halves apart. If this should prove difficult, sever with a razor blade where necessary. After the inside of the egg is cleaned and dry, remove the paraffin and you will have relatively clean-cut edges that you can perfect with bands of trimming.

If you want to cut the egg in half the long way, apply the band of paraffin as indicated. Then stick a pin in each end of the egg and tie a thread around them for a plumb line. You may mark this line or you may use the thread as a guide and prick it with the needle as before.

However you cut the eggshell apart, you will almost certainly wish to hinge the halves together. This is done by means of minute strips of adhesive tape, perhaps an eighth of an inch wide, stuck on in two places rather close together at what will become the back, or closed side. Exactly corresponding strips should be placed on the inside to complete and strengthen the hinges. The hinges should then be concealed either by painting or other trim, according to how you plan to decorate the whole egg.

For an oval inset, draw a pencil line of the oval exactly as you want it to be and, with a small pair of cuticle scissors, cut directly into the eggshell. This sort of cutting is almost sure-fire. And again, you need not remove the contents of the egg until you have completed the cutting.

LADDERS

A ladder is a very simple device for supporting any separate part of a decoupage in a shadow box not a part of the background. It could hardly be more primitive, yet sounds complicated in a description. It consists of a narrow strip of cardboard bent into a small, hollow, oblong shape and glued at the ends to stay that way. It can be from a quarter-inch to a half-inch wide, and of whatever length is necessary, say up to two or more inches high, depending upon what it is to support.

For a trial, take a strip of cardboard a quarter-inch wide and two inches long. Starting at one end, fold it in a quarter-inch. Make a second bend a quarter-inch beyond the first. Score these creases gently with a razor blade. Then measure 1¾ inches along your strip and make another bend. Repeat the quarter-inch fold beyond it, and score both creases. (Scoring makes the corners four-square and the whole ladder flat.) Now glue the ends together and you will have an oblong support, three-fourths of an inch long, a quarter-inch across top and bottom.

The long side of the ladder is, naturally, the perpendicular side. This is glued to the hedge or tree or figure it is to support, with their lower edges flush (otherwise the object would be off the floor). And, finally, this little wing or prop is glued to the hedge or tree or figure it is to support, with their lower edges flush so that they are well concealed.

Glossary

Adhesium glue size: a glutinous substance used to size a paper surface, not used as an adhesive in decoupage; especially good for spreading on the backs of cutouts with printed matter on them to prevent it from showing through when pasted up.

"Arte del uomo povero": poor man's art, or, *"arte del povero,"* art of the poor; furniture and accessories decorated with colorful prints and cutouts, pasted on and lacquered, chiefly from seventeenth- and eighteenth-century Venice; supposed to have been a cheap substitute for painted and lacquered furniture.

Carbon tetrachloride: chemical used as cleaning fluid or solvent under various trade names such as Carbona.

Cartouche: an ornamental device in a print, a tablet for inscription of place name or personage, often oval or oblong, sometimes in the form of a scroll.

Casein paints: opaque water colors, or tempera; color pigments are ground into water, a casein (milk curd) emulsion is used as a binder; fast-drying, waterproof, matte, and considered permanent.

Chinoiserie: designs, decoration in the Chinese taste; in prints, furniture, textiles such as *toiles de Jouy.* There were many establishments in France making *toiles,* some designed by Pillement.

Collage: a paste-up; a painting which incorporates cutouts of paper, newspaper, bits of string, wood, or any other random item that fits into the artist's conception of his composition; or a "painting" not of paint, made entirely of paper cutouts and other odd bits. (See Chapter 1.)

Cubism: a movement in painting which succeeded postimpressionism; initiated by Picasso and Braque in Paris about 1910, later followed by Gris, Duchamp and others; attempting expression in painting by use of geometrical shapes and figures, it was one of the earliest manifestations of abstract art.

Dada, Dadaism: a literary and art movement lasting only from about 1916 to 1922, chiefly in Europe; Dadaism reflected a rebellion against conventional art forms during and following World War I. It was iconoclastic and antirational, flouting accepted systems of government and society as well. Dadaists produced many of the early collages.

Dado: painting, papering or any similar decoration around the lower part of an interior wall different from the upper part.

Decoupage: a cutout, or cutouts used to make pictures, murals, shadow boxes, etc., or the decorating of surfaces, as furniture and accessories, to simulate painting (see Chapter 1).

"Decoupage chinois": term used by Lovina Kenyon to describe her particular style in decorating furniture and boxes with old Chinese papers.

"Découper": a French word meaning "to cut out"; used in the sense of a mechanical stamping out; also for carving, as of a fowl, or wood.

"Découpure": a French word meaning a "cutout"; also "cut paper work" (see Plate 3).

Dutch metal: metal leaf, a substitute for gold leaf and less expensive; made in Italy and Germany, Dutch metal is an alloy sold in square books ranging in size up to five inches; comes in several shades of gold, and in variegated tones of red and purple blended with brilliant green, each leaf between sheets of tissue. (For silver shade, use aluminum foil.)

Embossed gold paper trim: imported in strips and bands for cutting apart to decorate with as it comes, or to trim a decoupage; comes also in borders, bands, ornaments, numerals, alphabet, frames and corners. (See "Gold-Dec-It," Harrower Assoc., Sources of Supply.)

"Fêtes champêtres": an outdoor festival; a rural entertainment.

Flora: the collection of 1,000 "paper mosaic" flowers, or cutouts made by Mrs. Delany *c.*1775 and presented after her death to the British Museum (see Plates 21 and 22).

Fox paste: mixture of flour and water used by paper hangers to paste wallpaper on walls.

Foxed: to become discolored by decay or mildew, as old prints and old books.

Gilding: decorating with gold leaf; also with Dutch metal, an alloy (*q.v.*).

Gold size: a glutinous solution, sold in bottles and used as an adhesive for metal leaf (see Chapter 12).

Gouache: opaque colors, or tempera, for painting, which have been ground in water and mixed with a preparation of gum and sometimes honey.

Gutenberg, Johannes: German printer (*c.* 1398-1468) generally credited with the invention of movable type in the Western world; his first product, the Gutenberg Bible, begun in 1450.

Japan paints: sold in tubes and cans, japan colors are ground in quick-drying resinous varnish containing little or no oil; good for base surfaces for fast drying and require a protecting coat of clear, durable varnish.

Japanned, japanning: said of surfaces that have been varnished or lacquered; loosely, of varnishing or lacquering; originally, a special and unique hard-lacquered surface from Japan, usually thought of as black or red; japanning was the word used in England in the eighteenth and early nineteenth centuries for painted or varnished furniture, especially for furniture decorated with decoupage and lacquered. (See *"Ladies' Amusement".*)

Ladders: small devices made of narrow strips of cardboard and folded so as to support separate elements such as wings, props, figures, etc., in a deep shadow box or peep show.

"Ladies' Amusement, or The Whole Art of Japanning Made Easy": a book printed in London for Robert Sayer in 1760, containing two hundred sheets of hand-colored printed subjects to be cut out and pasted up for decorating furniture and other objects which then were japanned or lacquered. The book also contained about five pages of instructions on how to do this. (See Chapter 3.)

"L'Arte del uomo povero": see *"arte del uomo povero."*

Lurex: nontarnishing metallic yarn made by laminating aluminum foil or metalized film between two plies of clear plastic film; made in sheets and slit into yarn; can also be cut in strips; useful for added color and glitter in decoupages and murals.

Marbled, or marbleized: paper stained or colored to imitate marble (see Chapter 12).

"Merz": Kurt Schwitters' name for his collages to differentiate them from those of the early Dadaists in Germany.

Miter; mitering: a miter in decoupage is a small irregularly triangular snippet cut out of the covering fabric or paper at the corners (as of a box) when the covering is being applied, so that the edges of the material at corners can meet each other flat and flush; a "gusset" cut out to make an angle in a straight piece of material so that the resulting edges can be united.

Montage: a collage, a "mounting," composed of materials that may or may not be cutouts, often of identifiable objects superimposed. A montage may include photographs or photographic material, or be composed entirely of photographs; photomontage.

Ormolu: gilded bronze used in the decoration of furniture.

Paper mosaic: Mrs. Delany's name for her decoupaged Flora (*q.v.*).

Paper trim: see *Embossed gold paper trim.*

"Papiers collés": pasted papers; Picasso's name for his collages to distinguish them from the collages of the Dadaists.

"Papiers decoupés": cutout papers; Matisse's name for his collages and other paper cutouts.

"Pasta": Italian for farinaceous products such as macaroni, spaghetti.

Peep show: a home entertainment popular in the nineteenth century; consisted of vistas in miniature set up in a box and viewed through a peephole (see Chapter 3).

Pellon: a feltlike nonwoven fabric made with long staple fibers, bonded chemically and with heat; 70% nylon, 20% cotton, 10% acetate, durable and washable; can be cut in any direction without raveling, ideal for decoupage, in decorator colors.

Pinprick pictures: an ancient craft which became most popular in Europe in the eighteenth and early nineteenth centuries. Some pictures were made entirely with pinpricked paper designs or compositions; usually, prints already colored were pinpricked for added depth, to give them a rich, embossed look.

Photomontage: see *Montage.*

Potichomania: a fad for decorating glass vessels with decoupage to simulate ceramics such as Sèvres or Oriental vases.

Protectoid: plastic sheets, frosted on one side, that come in rolls about twenty inches wide; used for tracing from old books or prints so that the pressure of the pencil will not mark through.

Quillwork: an early European form of decoration used to embellish borders and other segments of pictures, wall sconces, heraldic devices; made by twisting small conelike spills of gilt paper, or vellum later colored or gilded. (See Chapter 12.)

Rottenstone: a powder, somewhat like pumice stone, made from decomposed siliceous limestone; used chiefly for polishing.

Sèvres: designation of a costly porcelain made at Sèvres, near Paris.

Shadow box: a decoupage, shell or artificial flower arrangement framed under glass in a boxlike frame, sometimes as deep as six inches or more.

Silhouette: an outline of a face, figure or other object cut out and filled in, usually with black. (See Chapter 1.)

Size, sizing: any of various glutinous substances for preparing surfaces such as paper, plaster or wood so that glue or paste will adhere when cutouts are applied; also to render surfaces waterproof.

Skeletonizing leaves: reducing leaves to skeletons, treating them so as to decompose the tissue between the veinings.

Stik-tacks: flat plastic discs, adhesive on both sides but easily detachable, in sizes from a dime to half that size; reusable, can be pared to any shape.

Surrealism: a serious movement in the art world which succeeded (and engulfed) Dadaism. Surrealism aimed in the realm of painting to overcome the barriers between the conscious and the unconscious; officially launched in 1924, and represented by such painters as Dali, Ernst, Miró, Tanguy, Magritte, who continued to some extent to use collage as a medium of expression.

Tinsel pictures: made as a fad during the early nineteenth century, tinsel pictures usually were prints representing well-known actors. Their costumes were decorated with cutout silks and garnished with tinsel or metal foil parts—helmets, breast plates, swords—stamped out by machine to fit in; sold in sets and pasted up for flamboyant pictures. (See Plates 20 and 66.)

"Toiles de Jouy": decorative fabrics (still widely copied) printed on linen or cotton from copper plates at Jouy, near Paris; typically in two-tone designs of rural scenes, farmsteads, ruins, with foliage and rivers, bridges, boats, etc., in chinoiserie style in characteristic red, green, blue or brown on cream color. There were many establishments similar to the one at Jouy throughout France at that time.

Trim: see *embossed gold paper trim.*

"Trompe l'oeil": a "fool-the-eye" technique in painting; a still-life representation of objects so exact as to create the illusion of reality; *trompe l'oeil* effects with cutouts widely used in decoupage (see Plates 5, 54 and 55).

"Vues d'optiques": printed and colored representations of scenes, vistas, or spectacles designed to exaggerate the effects of perspective; popular in the eighteenth and nineteenth centuries; the word *optique* implies "optical illusion."

Wood filler: can be a liquid or a malleable substance such as putty for filling in pits or flaws on a wood surface before painting it; old hands at renovating wood surfaces for decoupage prefer a "paste" which comes as a powder and is diluted with water for the desired consistency.

Sources of Supply

SHOPS AND shopping areas differ from one community to another. There will always be the element of adventure in collecting the things you need for decoupage, especially since your requirements may vary widely from project to project to include much that is unpredictable and irrelevant to available market places. The following suggestions are given with the knowledge that you will have to explore your own shopping facilities. This listing should provide, particularly in the New York area, at least a guide for happy hunting.

Antique shops: prints, old papers and books; shells, stones; scraps of fabric; milk-glass eggs, small ornament or picture frames — things too numerous to mention, depending upon luck and locality.

Art stores: prints, old and new; books for cutting up. Many art shops combine books with pictures; a good source for frames, too.

Art-supply stores:
Books, art
Brushes; painting knives, spatulas
X-acto knives
Gold leaf, Dutch metal, gold size
Glues and pastes, standard makes such as Sobo, Elmer's glue, DuPont Duco cement.
Paints: oils, water colors, casein colors, gouache, japan colors; some lacquers, varnishes (also varnish and paint removers); turpentine and other solvents
Papers: cardboard, construction paper, drawing paper, masking tape, sandpaper, tracing paper, waxed carbon paper
Pencils: charcoal sticks
Plastics: Stik-tacks, Protectoid, Traceolene

Bookstores: books, magazines, prints. Many bookstores have print departments, just as some art stores carry books. In New York see:

Argosy, 114 East 59th St.

Brentano, 586 Fifth Ave.

Brown & Delhi, 57 Fifth Ave.

Dauber & Pine, 66 Fifth Ave.

Goldschmidt, Lucien, 1116 Madison Ave., (prints, rare books)

Schatzki, Walter, 125 East 56th St., (old prints, rare books)

The Old Print Shop, 150 Lexington Ave.

Weyhe, E. 794 Lexington Ave., (art books, old prints)

Also, Book Row, in lower Fourth Ave., below 14th St. to Astor Place, for secondhand books, prints, posters, lithographs, maps, Americana:

Arcadia Bookshop

Atlantis Bookshop

Pageant Book Company

Vanity Fair

Weiser, Samuel, and many others

Department stores:

Decorative papers, wallpapers (some)

Decorative fabrics

Pellon

Some department stores have sections devoted to prints and to books. Large department stores carry hardware, paints and brushes, varnish, lacquer, paint remover and other supplies for painting and decorating. Others have craft and stationery departments with such supplies as papers, pastes, Exacto knives and various art supplies.

Dime stores, drug and variety stores: around the corner from almost any dwelling in America is a local shop—or shops—which offers many of the incidental and minor necessities for decoupage. Just for a sampling: hardware items, paints and brushes, rubber gloves, lace doilies, pastes, glues, solvents, steel wool, Carbona, cuticle scissors, razor blades, tweezers, and countless other items which, quite likely, are already resting on your cupboard shelves.

Glass dealers: sheet glass, plate glass, glass tops (see your local telephone company "Red Book.")

Hardware and/or paint stores:
    Adhesium glue size, shellac and other sizings
    Emery cloth
    Glass (some hardware stores)
    Lacquers; spray guns
    Paints and brushes; paint remover
    Rottenstone
    Rust remover
    Sandpaper
    Scissors
    Scratch Fixing Liquid
    Steel wool
    Tools
    Turpentine and other solvents
    Varnishes; varnish remover
    Wallpaper (some paint stores); fox paste
    Wallpaper roller
    Wood filler

Specialties:
    Dennison, 411 Fifth Avenue, New York:
    Crepe paper in "artists" colors
    Decorative papers
    Embossed gold paper trim
    Felt
    Paper lace, doilies
    Standard glues and pastes
    Stik-tacks

Gregory, K., 222 East 71st Street. By appointment only.

Prints, chiefly French and English, eighteenth century, early nineteenth, florals, fruits, views, costumes

Marbled and other decorative papers

Embossed gold paper trim

Hill Company, 61 East 45th Street

Book-Saver, water-soluble paste with polyvinal acetate base, adhesive for all paper and cloth paste-ups

Harrower Associates, 34 East 10th Street

Embossed gold paper trim

Prints: French and English, hand-colored, scenics and old English houses; florals; fashion prints—Ackermann's, Godey's, Graham's Magazine

Eggs: milk-glass, papier-mâché, plastic

Boxes, wood and plastic

Selection of pearls and colored stones

Sobo, water-soluble paste

Laverne Originals, 160 East 57th Street

Decorative papers—marbled, textured, tortoise-shell, etc.

Larsen, H. K., Company, North Webster, Indiana

Special paints in gold, silver, ivory white, jet black, in half-pint cans. Write for price list.

Lurex: apply *The Dobeckmun Company,* 350 Fifth Avenue, New York for retail outlet or jobber if not obtainable locally.

Nelson-Whitehead Paper Corp., 7 Laight Street, New York

Imported and domestic decorative papers of all types—marbled, malachite, colored, textured, etc.

Shells: beaches; antique shops; shell shops such as McArthur's, 144 East 61st Street in New York; also Shell Clubs, of which there are many. (In New York the New York Shell Club meets monthly at the American Museum of Natural History.)

Index